A Transcendental Journey

Stephen Evans

This book is dedicated to my father, who taught me, among so many things, to drive.

This is a work of memory and imagination. And memory is imagination in reverse.

Copyright © 2022 by Stephen Evans. All rights reserved.

Book Layout ©2017 BookDesignTemplates.com

A Transcendental Journey: Stephen Evans; Twenty-Fifth Anniversary edition.

ISBN: 978-1-953725-28-8

Time Being Media LLC

"We are now so far from the road to truth, that religious teachers dispute and hate each other, and speculative men are esteemed unsound and frivolous."

— Ralph Waldo Emerson

Afterword Part I

The weather in Concord, Massachusetts was freezing. Snow flittered to the ground. It didn't matter. It was my birthday. My present to myself was seeing Walden Pond.

I drove carefully through the slush that covered Walden Road, past the snow-silent shops of Sunday Concord and out into the lightly wooded countryside. Only a mile or so down the two-lane road, I rolled slowly into the unplowed parking lot at Walden Pond State Park.

In the summer, the parking lot filled up early. More than two million people, tourists, locals, and pilgrims like me, visited Walden each year. But that day, the parking lot was nearly empty. Even the New Englanders were being more sensible than I was.

I shuffled across the lot and past a tiny cabin-like structure, a model of a long ago residence. Ralph Waldo Emerson once owned some land by Walden Pond. In 1844, he let a young friend and protégé named Henry David Thoreau build a one-room cabin in a clearing by the north shore.

Slipping past the Ranger Station/Visitor Center/Gift Shop, I glanced down the empty road, skidded gracelessly across, and tramped down the slight decline to the shore of the pond. At the edge of the water, I paused.

I had seen the picture many times. But the pond was larger than I expected, half a mile across maybe. Ice covered all the watery surface, no telling how thick. Snow obscured any evidence of skating or other winter activities.

A wide swath of trees encircled the shore, crowding down to the waterline in all but a few spots. I examined the shoreline, fractal, like mountains, trees, clouds, and snowflakes; similar designs and patterns occurred over and over at varying scales. Standing by the frozen shoreline, I couldn't see any patterns, just a rough wide circle with an occasional dip in or out.

On my right, an asphalt path led into the encircling woods. I knew its history. The path had been laid over an old forest trail, one that Emerson and Thoreau might well have followed as they charted a site for the cabin. They were both great walkers, and their conversations on the march through the Massachusetts countryside ranged from Plato to pines, gardens to Goethe.

An inch of snow lay undisturbed over the path. The sky, more thick white than gray, showed no sign of clearing. But I ignored the weather and began to walk (or skate really in leather-soled loafers), counterclockwise from over the pond looking down or clockwise from under the pond looking up. The frigid silence was breathtaking. I began to shiver, my slim faux-leather jacket little protection against the wind. I walked faster.

About a third of the way around the path, a small clearing opened up in the woods. More than one hundred and fifty years earlier, Thoreau had erected his cabin there. I stood silent, listening for the natural music that Thoreau might have heard on a similar winter's day.

Instead, I heard the clatter and chatter of a troop of high school girls surging into the clearing from the other direction. They quickly flooded the cabin site, chattering and taking pictures and chattering more and taking more pictures. Then in a blink and a flash, they vanished like spirits at dawn, shivering and chattering the other way around the pond.

The snow was falling much harder, drawing a lace curtain around the clearing. Determined to complete the circuit, I continued along the path, hurrying as much as possible on the slippery surface. A little past the halfway point, where the trail neared the frozen edge of the pond, I came to a halt. The path was closed, fenced off and posted with warning signs.

I looked out over the icy surface, pondering my choices. I could return the way I had come, chancing another encounter with the high school girls. Or I could set off into the woods and try to find a way through.

Flakes like goose down were starting to flutter around me, merging into the inches now on the ground. The wind was brisk, the chill near zero. Still I took the woods.

My porous soggy jacket began to freeze. Snow crept into my loafers. Frigid wet oozed through my socks. Skating the path became trudging through woods. In the exertion, pain spread through my chest, my breathing forced and halting. I thought of the Frost poem "Stopping by Woods on a Snowy Evening". Whoever was smart not to go in.

Bracken and branches drove me away from the shoreline. My circle around the pond curved wider, drifting, I guessed, toward Emerson's cliff, a ridge several hundred yards from the edge of the pond.

Everywhere was thick with snow. Soon the pond disappeared altogether behind a wall of snowbound trees. I wandered blindly, unable to see or hear anyone. My body ached up and down from the cold, but the pain sprouting in my chest was sharper, shallow wheezing breaths all I could manage.

Sit, I thought.

Catch.

Breath.

Try not to die alone in a park visited by millions.

I shook my head and smiled. How foolish! What had possessed me to come out on a day like this? Why had I wandered off into the woods instead of taking the easy path back? Why was I so drawn to Walden and Concord and Emerson?

Had I been Ralph Waldo Emerson in a past life?

Had my spirit walked the paths of Walden all those years ago?

Was delirious speculation a symptom of frostbite?

I laughed and laughed, until the snow around my feet began to melt.

Chapter One

Self-Reliance

We live on the surface of the past. In the millisecond it takes electrochemical fact to scurry from eye (or skin or tongue) to brain, the present has danced away.

Now, then.

Now, then.

Every fact is a memory.

*
*
*

The movie was *Contact*, based on a book by Astronomer to the Stars Carl Sagan. A scientist (played by the lovely and talented actress Jodie Foster) intercepts a message from aliens. The coded missive contains blueprints for building an intergalactic transporter that teleports her to a galaxy far far away where she is enlightened by mysterious beings and returned to Earth. But no one believes her story.

After the movie, I left the theater and walked to my car beside the steaming pavement, glistening wet under metallic pink street lights from the earlier rain. Sometime during the film, I realized, I had made a decision. I was going a journey of my own.

Not to see aliens (necessarily). To write a book. A Carl Sagan-type book. I called myself a writer. I had written some poetry, a few stories, a play. I had never written a book. Maybe I could.

But where would I go?

*
*
*

For last two years of my marriage, I was lost.

We had moved from my home just outside Washington DC to her adopted home of Minneapolis. I came to love the city, but for some reason had a hard time finding my way. I could locate the dry cleaners at one end of our street, the lake at the other end, the grocery which was that way on Hennepin Avenue, and the coffee shop which was the other way. That was about it.

In my car I had an old Rand-McNally book of state maps. I had bought it when I drove up to my new home. The Minnesota state map had a small insert for Minneapolis, and after the move I consulted it often. On the first page of the book (two pages really, across the fold) there was a map of the entire country.

Maybe you know this, but I didn't at the time. The Federal Highway system uses even numbers for highways going east-west and odd numbers for highways going north-south. The largest east-west interstates have numbers that end in zero. I-90 is the northernmost of these highways.

I-90 passes about 100 miles south of Minneapolis, extending in almost a straight line to Yellowstone, then on to the Pacific Ocean. That line on the map called to me, even after the divorce and I left Minnesota and moved back to Washington DC. I-90 for me was The Road Not Taken.

So I thought about that Rand-McNally map and that line that led to the far ocean. And I formed a plan. My plan was not to plan. I would drive wherever I-90 and my 1992 Teal Blue Chevy Cavalier took me.

During the day, I would explore natural wonders, places I had always wanted to see, like Yellowstone and...whatever was on the way to Yellowstone. At night, alone in the light of the Western stars, I would compose my long-imagined opus exploring the philosophical ramifications of quantum mechanics.

A best-seller for sure.

I quit my job and set out on the road, kerowacking across the country with no agenda, no timeframe, and no certainty of return.

From DC, I drove north and west, junction by junction ascending the national highway system until I reached Minneapolis. I took a brief hiatus (lunch with my ex in Stillwater, dinner with my cousins in St. Paul). The next morning marked the real beginning of my journey. The idea was to head south on I-35 until I hit I-90 at Albert Lea.

I started my Cavalier, hit the gas, and turned to look behind me. For future reference, I do not recommend performing those actions in that particular order. Fortunately for the children playing in the street behind me, a warning siren loud enough to shake the windows of my car blasted the air, causing the kids to scatter (I choose to blame the siren and not my driving) and me to hit the brakes.

Universally a siren signals a disaster, an air raid or mine collapse. In the mid-west, it usually means a tornado. In the two years I lived in Minneapolis, I had heard the siren once or twice, but I had never seen a tornado. But my Iowa-born father had taught me what to look for. Low on the south-west horizon, I spotted a small purple-black cloud.

The cyclone seedling took evasive action, but somehow I managed to track straight for it. Finally I confronted the errant tempest on the bridge that spans the Minnesota River just a few miles south of Minneapolis. A sudden torrent dropped visibility to near zero and engulfed the highway. My Cavalier toiled slowly but diligently through the flood. Shrouded lights white and red fore and aft glimpsed through the glooming spray were the only sign of progress. In the middle of the bridge (as best I could tell), I glanced over the rail and down at the river supposedly below. Streaming dark grey clouds had swallowed the river. In Minnesota, the Liquid State, everything flows into everything.

Avoiding obscure oncoming beams of white, trailing vague and distant red beacons, I crossed the invisible bridge. On the other side, the curtain parted as the tempest raced away behind me.

After escaping the deluge, I turned off I-35 and postponed my I-90 rendezvous, stopping to regroup at Mystic Lake casino. It may seem like an odd choice for a rest stop, but the place had been a haven to me. Toward the end of my marriage, I often spent Saturday afternoons at Mystic Lake, buying a few dollars of peace among the swirling lights and clanging bells.

Smaller than Las Vegas and friendlier than Atlantic City, Mystic Lake was the largest and most successful casino in Minnesota. The casino and hotel are owned by a community of the Dakota Indian nation, the Shakopee Mdewakanton (pronounced just the way it sounds). The place was pleasant and well-run, with reasonably priced food, friendly service, and decent returns in the slot machines (it took longer to lose your money). Substantial income from the operation was distributed to the local Indian community, which like many such communities across the country had historically experienced high levels of poverty. So it seemed a good deal all around, in my view.

The casino was named after nearby Mystic Lake, which I imagined was the pleasant little pond just visible from the road. I never saw anything mystical about it. But then speeding down to a casino may not produce the proper mind frame for spiritual observation. I stayed that day just long enough to have lunch and drop fifty bucks or so in the whirling digital dervishes. Then I was off again.

Invoking Pythagoras, I opted for a short cut across the hypotenuse of the state. Instead of taking the major highways, I tracked the Minnesota River down Route 169 to Mankato, the Twin Cities favorite cousin maybe eighty miles southwest of Minneapolis. Then I angled off on smaller roads, winding my way around and through the broad Blue Earth country of southern Minnesota.

Blue Earth doesn't refer to the soil, which is the same rich black prairie loam my father farmed as a boy. The name derives from the blue-green clay used in religious ceremonies by the local Dakota tribe.

But this was definitely my father's Midwest. Two-lane roads coursed through undulating oceans of wheat and soy, bridged by fleeting main street towns of pureblood vowels and pickup trucks armored with September snowplows.

I was starting to calm down after the frantic morning escape, in part because of the pastoral tranquility of the countryside, appealing even in the diffuse glow that illuminated the overcast day, and also because I almost never saw a car on my side of the road. Nearly everyone else that day was traveling in the opposite direction. I wondered what were they escaping from, or what I was escaping to.

Or should I say we?

There is a great literary tradition of animals as traveling companions. Steinbeck crossed America with a poodle named Charlie. Dante explored Paradise with a clairvoyant Saint Bernard.

My companion, also named Bernard, was a toy moose about eight inches tall with brown fur and auburn antlers. I had a thought that someday I might write a children's book about his adventures. I have snapshots of Bernard climbing Devil's Tower in Wyoming, searching for relatives in the marshes of Yellowstone, peering out over the Colorado Mountains.

But he spent most of the voyage sitting in the passenger seat on top of my knapsack, which was just high enough that he could peek out, but not so high that I would be stopped by the Highway Patrol (or so I thought).

The knapsack generally contained reading material (more on that later), my laptop computer, and sometimes Bernard, who would pop inside when I would go into McDonalds for a nutritionally balanced breakfast of French Fries and SUPERSIZE coke. (Throughout this book, I have tried to report accurately on the size of the soft drinks I purchased, because I wanted to report accurately on something.)

A fellow vegetarian, Bernard would sometimes try to talk me out of McDonalds. Though actually Bernard didn't speak; he just curled his antlers in disdain. For meaningful silence, there's no one like a toy moose.

Since Bernard was not much for conversation, there wasn't a lot to do as I meandered along the highway.

Gaze out the window.

Snack on French Fries.

Try to sing.

In Ninth grade, I had to choose between Chorus and Shop. Chorus had lots of girls. Shop had no girls. It was an easy choice.

In Tenth grade, I got drafted into the spring musical, but agreeably, again on the Follow the Girls theory.

By the time I graduated from college, I was studying voice privately and considering a career in opera. Eventually, I decided that being a professional singer was too insecure a career choice (writing being so much more stable). But over the years I had performed frequently in musical theater, with the occasional operetta or classical recital.

On the road, I began planning a new One-Man Show consisting exclusively of songs I had always wanted to sing but hadn't for various reasons. I devised lists in different categories. Songs for tenors (I'm a baritone). Songs for women (I'm a baritone). Songs I was too young for (fewer and fewer). Songs I was too old for (more and more). The planning was going well, except for one problem.

I couldn't sing anymore.

I could speak. I could even sing in a group. But when I tried to sing solo, the muscles in my throat would clench up as soon as the first phrase crossed my lips.

Sad songs were hard.

Happy songs were worse.

The music tunneled down where nothing else could reach. Then something rode up with the breath and strangled my vocal chords. I was literally choked with emotion.

The psychological term for this phenomenon is Conversion Reaction or Conversion Disorder, a physical manifestation of an emotional trauma. I had heard of people who had suffered some terrible event and lost their ability to speak or walk or see. But I had never heard of anyone who couldn't sing.

Oddly, the last time I had sung in public was at my own wedding. After the wedding, I stopped singing. I had no time for it. Then as the marriage began to wither, so did my desire to sing. After the divorce, I discovered that my voice had withered too. Here's a marriage tip from someone who shouldn't give them: Never let yourself go. You may not find yourself again.

Cognitive Musicology investigates the emotional and physiological aspects of music. We have discovered in recent years that music stimulates widely different areas of the brain, from those related to language processing all the way down to the limbic system, a primordial area of the brain where our most fundamental emotional reactions occur (which makes sense, when you remember that birds and whales have been singing millions of years longer than humans).

I thought about finding a cognitive musicologist and offering myself as a subject of study: The Singer who couldn't Sing. Might have been worth a footnote in someone's dissertation. But I never told anyone. I just stopped singing.

When you are a writer, or even when you just call yourself one, you learn to respect the words that pop up suddenly in your mind. It's a kind of celestial dictation. Since I couldn't sing to pass the time and Bernard was not one for chit chat, I mostly spent the day in silence. Occasionally, something curious would catch my eye or a momentary insight would tap me on the shoulder and I'd reach into my knapsack, pull out a little silver mini-tape recorder, and record the moment for posterity. Here are some examples:

"Immortality comes from what we teach."

"I've been seeing signs for waffle houses."

"I sure hope this tape is working."

I disproved the Pythagorean Theorem that day, as my short cut increased my travel time by several hours. And mile after mile, as the Minnesota landscape approached and receded, recurring blurs of fence posts and mailboxes and telephone poles mesmerized me.

Along the roadside, hordes of white or yellow butterflies danced like transmigrated souls uncertain in their delicate new incarnation. As I watched, the words *death by butterfly wings* began fluttering through my head.

I recorded the phrase *death by butterfly wings*, though the image startled me. What could possibly associate such lovely serene creatures with death? Was it prophecy? Dream? Sleep deprivation?

I had no answer, then. But soon, my butterfly daydreams faded behind me and as farms and fields whipped past my window, the state line beckoned. By early evening, I crossed the line into South Dakota without a glimmer of regret. I was on to something.

*
*
*

It was still pretty light, one of the perks of the latitude. But I had come far enough for the first day, so I sought refuge in Sioux Falls. I ventured a quick spin around the city, then settled on a small motel in a commercial strip just off the interstate, preparing for an early getaway. Boxy bar/casinos with lost-letter neon signs surrounded me. But I wasn't tempted to try my luck again. I just hauled my suitcase, knapsack, and Bernard out of the car.

And a book.

As I was preparing for the trip, I had packed to the brim a one-foot square box of books. For the first half of the journey, the box stayed in the back seat, where I could grab a volume anytime I needed to peruse something at highway speeds. About half way through the trip, the box migrated to the trunk to provide ballast in case of snow in the mountain passes.

Most of the books in the box were research for the one I was planning to write, with subjects like quantum physics, relativity, string theory, complexity theory, and so forth (a best-seller for sure.) But for my own reading pleasure, I brought three books.

Walden by Henry David Thoreau was the first. Since I was going to see Nature, Thoreau seemed the proper choice. I had read *Walden* several times. Thoreau's elegant prose, sly and stern, always delighted and inspired. And in a way, I was following his prescription of *Simplicity, Simplicity, Simplicity!*

Zen and the Art of Motorcycle Maintenance was the second book. During my senior year in college, the magenta and yellow paperbacks had festooned bookstore racks like Day-Glo wallpaper. After slogging through Heidegger and Faulkner during the day, my late night sittings were devoted to Robert Pirsig's radical demolition of western rationality and his protagonist's sanity. I wanted to read it again, now that I had more experience in personal destruction. Plus, I was driving across country, so the maintenance hints might come in handy.

The third book I choose was *Essays* by Ralph Waldo Emerson. The gold and green Spencer Press edition had been sitting around my mother's house for years. The book was still in good condition, probably from decades of not being opened.

I had never read Emerson. But I knew that he had some connection to Thoreau, so I threw the book in the box.

In Sioux Falls that night, I thought about starting to write my Carl Sagan book. But all I really wanted was some good short bedtime reading. That left out *Zen*. *Walden* can be read in short bursts, but I had read it often. The Emerson essays were only about thirty pages each, so I took the book with me into the motel room.

Ralph Waldo Emerson was born in Boston on May 25, 1803. At age 14 he entered Harvard and by 18 he was teaching school. In 1829, Waldo (the name he preferred) was ordained a minister at the Second Unitarian Church in Boston, after which he soon married the spirited Ellen Tucker. Their happiness was brief, as she died of tuberculosis less than two years later.

After his wife's death, Emerson resigned his ministry and wandered through Europe for nearly a year. On his return home, Emerson moved a few miles outside Boston to Concord, Massachusetts, where his grandfather, the local Unitarian minister, had organized the defense of the Old North Bridge in 1775. Waldo soon married his second wife, Lidian, and began his new work.

Faced with a need to earn a living, Emerson chose a career as a lecturer. Lectures in the 1830s were what PBS is today. Emerson wrote extensive daily journals, which became source material for his lectures. The lectures were then edited for publication, becoming the essays.

In the years between 1836 and 1838, Emerson published a short pamphlet entitled *Nature*, and gave two speeches now known as *The American Scholar*, and *The Divinity School Address*. In 1841, Emerson published his first series of essays. A second series was published three years later.

These works shook the comfortable Eurocentric foundations of American intellectual and religious thought. And in less than a decade, the former Unitarian minister had reshaped American philosophical discourse and forged the spiritual consciousness of the youthful nation. In the process, Emerson had transformed himself, from religious rebel to international sage, and into the founder of the Nineteenth century philosophy known as American Transcendentalism.

The Transcendentalist movement, if such a chaotic collection of ideas and ideologues could be called one, was centered in Emerson's home town of Concord. Cohorts Henry David Thoreau, Bronson Alcott (now known primarily as the father of Louisa May), William Ellery Channing, and Margaret Fuller comprised a Transcendental intelligentsia revolving around Emerson's powerful personality.

Emerson also influenced popular writers of the day such as Nathaniel Hawthorne (Emerson's sometime walking companion, who lived just down the Lexington road) and Herman Melville, as well as the unpopular (Walt Whitman), and the nonpopular (Emily Dickinson).

My Spencer Press edition of *Emerson's Essays* mixed and matched from the two series of essays of 1841 and 1844. Emerson's most famous essays were represented, including *The Poet*, *The Over-Soul*, and *Self-Reliance*.

In Sioux Falls that night, I flopped onto the jouncy mattress, switched on the small bedside lamp, and flipped through most of the book. Then I settled in to read the one essay I had heard of: *Self-Reliance*.

Self-Reliance starts with a Latin quote I couldn't translate, then another few lines from a couple of Elizabethan playwrights whom I had never read, followed by a bit of obscure poetry about bantlings on the rocks. I wasn't encouraged and almost stopped reading. But then Emerson relates a chatty anecdote:

> *"I read the other day some verses written by an eminent painter which were original and not conventional. The soul always hears an admonition in such lines, let the subject be what it may. The sentiment they instill is of more value than any thought they may contain."*

He follows this friendly counsel with this phrase:

> *"To believe your own thought, to believe that what is true for you in your private heart is true for all men,—that is genius."*

I sat up and pulled the lamp closer to the bed, tilting the shade up to get more light. I had the odd impression that I was not reading an essay written 150 years earlier, but a letter written to me. I read the phrase again.

> *"To believe your own thought, to believe that what is true for you in your private heart is true for all men,—that is genius."*

I kept reading. Further down I came to this:

> *"I would write on the lintels of the door-post, 'Whim'. I hope it is somewhat better than whim at last, but we cannot spend the day in explanation."*

Whim. Hope. Yes.

I kept reading and stopping, reading and stopping, the words detonating inside me. The prose was all roundhouse, fists flying in every phrase:

> *"Trust thyself: every heart vibrates to that iron string."*
> *"Whoso would be a man, must be a nonconformist."*
> *"Nothing is at last sacred but the integrity of your own mind."*

"I do not wish to expiate, but to live."
"A foolish consistency is the hobgoblin of little minds."
"To be great is to be misunderstood."
"Every true man is a cause, a country, and an age;"

Finally I came to the end and read:

"Nothing can bring you peace but yourself. Nothing can bring you peace but the triumph of principles."

I closed the book, and set it on the bedtable.

Past roads were closed off.

No clear route lay ahead.

But in Ralph Waldo Emerson, I knew I had a found a guide into unfamiliar states.

*
*
*

When you decide what you are looking for, you decide what you can find.

I woke late the next morning and ambled over to the waffle shop next door, waffles having been on my mind for several states. Plus I needed coffee to cut through my groggy transcendental self-awareness.

Outside the shop, I paused to pick up a paper. A local newspaper is a fifty-cent university, mapping the mythology of small town life. Each day on my journey I read America shorthand.

The newspaper for Sioux Falls was the Argus Leader. The mythological Argus—called Panoptes, or all-seeing—was an Arcadian monster-hero, blessed or cursed with a hundred eyes. According to legend, the Trickster God Hermes lulled Argus to sleep one day (no small feat to shut so many eyes), then absconded with Zeus' human lover Io, who for her own protection was transformed into a cow (I have occasionally wondered how that conversation went). On Argus' death, his eyes ended up on the tail of a peacock which ended up on the tail of a television network.

So Argus, the all-seeing guardian who fell asleep on the job, is a natural if unusually honest name for a newspaper. It's also a popular name. In addition to the Sioux Falls Argus Leader, there's the Press Argus-Courier of Van Buren, Arkansas; the Current-Argus of Carlsbad, New

Mexico; the Argus of Fremont, California; the Argus-Courier of Petaluma, California, and many others.

After finishing breakfast and the Argus Leader, I sat drinking good coffee (a tradition at waffle houses) and contemplating my next move.

When I started planning my trip, several people (okay, two) mentioned that the National Monument in Pipestone, Minnesota, was worth seeing. Though I was a certified former resident of Minnesota, this surprised me. I had never heard of Pipestone. And strangely, no one could ever really explain to me what Pipestone National Monument was a monument to. So I was curious. And it was only a few hours away. But it was back in Minnesota.

So I wondered. Should I go back? It felt wrong to backtrack so soon in the trip. It felt wrong to head back into Minnesota at all. It felt very wrong to have to think so much before noon.

Someone once said that sometimes you have to go backward to go forward. If they didn't, well, then it ruins my anecdote. Anyway, whoever said it has no sense of direction. But maybe they have a hundred eyes.

I left Sioux Falls, backtracked fifty miles or so on I-90, then headed north a ways on Minnesota Route 75. Soon Bernard and I rolled into the village of Pipestone.

Imagine a small Midwestern town of about 5000 people, too big for everyone to know everyone, but not too big for everyone to want to know everyone. That was Pipestone. I'm sure bad things happened there. But it felt like they didn't.

In town, I turned toward the McDonalds. I can always find a McDonalds—that is my sixth sense. Bernard and I grabbed some french fries and a SUPERSIZE coke, out of habit more than hunger.

It was a clear hot weekend morning and the restaurant was filled with mini-gangs in Soccer uniforms. The noise was deafening. And heartening.

Slightly intoxicated by the sounds of small town Saturday, I drove a few blocks into the heart of Pipestone. Signs guided me (street signs, not mystical portents) as I combed the village for Federal Institutions. Once, twice, three times, I drove up and down, end to end, on the street where the monument was supposed to be.

I found the city hall. I found the library. I found the museum. I found a tall church built from dark red stone, and the sun-blanched rickety remains of a wooden frame paddock or enclosure. But I couldn't find a monument. Any monument.

I had lived most of my life near Washington DC, so I knew what monuments looked like. Monuments were tall and pointy-shaped like...a monument. You can't miss the Washington monument.

So I drove all over Pipestone looking for something carved in marble, draped in bunting, illuminated by eternal flames with brass plaques on the walls intoning interminable phrases (like this one). There were none to be found.

Finally, I returned to McBaseCamp. Bernard and I soothed our frustration with more french fries and another SUPERSIZE coke. The Soccer gangs had been replaced by adolescent gender-segregated hordes in skateboard giggling mode.

I munched in my corner and pondered reasons to leave. I was frustrated. I was still in Minnesota. Pipestone was a pipe dream.

Nevertheless, Coke in hand, I again went out again. Why? There's that old joke:

> *Q: Why are things lost always in the last place you look?*
> *A: Because you stop looking when you find them.*

Maybe the answer should be:

Because you only find them when you stop looking.

But then it wouldn't be a joke.

Not expecting to find anything, but also not willing to betray my gender by asking directions, I wandered the same roads as before, encountered the same buildings, and sometimes the same people, who probably concluded that I was casing the city but felt secure in the knowledge that no Outsider could ever descry their monument.

I slowed once more as I drove by the same tumbledown wooden structure I had seen before. Timbers withered and blanched by wind and snow somehow managed to remain upright. It was old certainly, maybe the remnant of a small fort, or a frontier trading post. But it certainly didn't look like a monument.

It wasn't. On the other side of the street, a sign three feet high in a wide-open field stated in bold red letters:

Pipestone National Monument

I had missed the sign six, maybe eight times, fascinated each time by the dilapidated fort. Tricky of these inscrutable Midwesterners to hide their monument behind a sign.

Laughing at my observational skills (or lack thereof), I zipped without looking across the road. Massive boulders guarded the entrance, deposited so the rumor goes by a retreating glacier.

(That glacier seems to shoulder a lot of blame thereabouts. There is a theory that a glacier created the ten thousand lakes of Minnesota. But this story that seems less than credible to me. Never once during my two-year residence did a mile-high wall of ice come down from Canada.)

I drove up the asphalt driveway curving though a long grassy field and parked in front of a brown-green one-story government-issue building that looked like a small school or the Motor Vehicle Administration. No marble was anywhere to be seen.

The nondescript building in front of me didn't seem likely to be worth the time and effort I had expended to find it. But I was so grateful to have finally found something that I wasn't about to leave without checking it out. So I loaded Bernard and the camera into my knapsack and trudged into the building.

As I stepped inside, a woman grabbed me and rushed me through some curtains into a darkened room. Normally, that would have been the highlight of my day. But by then it just added to the mystery that was Pipestone.

I had only missed a few minutes, the enigmatic figure whispered, without explaining a few minutes of what. Then she slipped a brochure into my hand, assuming apparently that I could read in the dark.

It turned out that the few minutes belonged to a slide show, something I hadn't seen since elementary school. The presentation was sponsored by some industrial company (I don't remember which), so obviously the government was not pumping hordes of money into Pipestone. Maybe it was a really small monument. Yet despite the low-tech medium, the display was entertaining and informative, presenting both the natural and cultural history of Pipestone.

Pipestone was named for a kind of stone, a unique sedimentary rock created when thousands of years of pressure from that ubiquitous glacier compressed the underlying red clay. The pipestone itself is covered by a layer of quartzite, the dark red stone on the town buildings. The quartzite layer can be as much as eight feet deep and is one of the hardest known minerals.

For hundreds of years, Native Americans of many tribes have been mining the quarries at Pipestone, and carving the soft stone into ceremonial pipes and other artifacts. These tribes consider the Pipestone quarries sacred ground. Only Native Americans are permitted to quarry pipestone and only traditional tools may be used. Mining pipestone is backbreaking work.

Pipestone is also known as Catlinite. At least, it's been known as Catlinite since a frontier artist named George Catlin heard about the quarries and traveled down to investigate. Native Americans probably have their own name for the mineral, which probably translates sensibly to pipestone.

In 1836, the same year that Emerson published *Nature*, Catlin recorded the legend of Pipestone in his *Account of a Journey to the Coteau des Prairies*:

"At an ancient time the Great Spirit, in the form of a large bird, stood upon the wall of rock and called all the tribes around him, and breaking out a piece of the red stone formed it into a pipe and smoked it, the smoke rolling over the whole multitude. He then told his red children that this red stone was their flesh, that they were made from it, that they must all smoke to him through it, that they must use it for nothing but pipes: and as it belonged alike to all tribes, the ground was sacred, and no weapons must be used or brought upon it."

In 1928, the Federal Government bought the land from the Yankton Sioux, who no longer found the property convenient, having been relocated to a reservation 150 miles away. Nine years later, the land was designated Pipestone National Monument.

When the slide show was over, I walked out of the back door of the building (which as it turned out was the Pipestone visitors center). A narrow asphalt path wound its way into a sparse wood. The trees of medium height showed no hint yet of fall colors (autumn in Minnesota is measured in heartbeats).

The glare of the sun was blinding after the dark room, so I wandered into the meager shade of the trees to examine the brochure. The booklet retold the story of Pipestone, and provided a map and guide to the grounds. Because that's what the monument really was, not a marble construct, but three hundred acres of prairie grasslands. Pipestone is one of the few remaining preserves in Minnesota of Mixed Prairie Grassland, the ecological term for Really Tall Weeds.

I now know that, for the Federal Government, the word 'monument' stands for more than a man-made edifice. According to the Federal Antiquities Act of 1906, monuments are "landmarks, structures, and other objects of historic or scientific interest situated on lands owned or controlled by the government" that are declared by public proclamation of the President to be national monuments. Basically, if the Feds own it and the President says so, it's a monument.

The Government also has different designations for parks, memorials, preserves, and so on. Here are the official definitions from the National Park Service:

National Parks are generally large natural areas having a wide variety of attributes, at times including significant historic assets. Hunting, mining and consumptive activities are not authorized.

National Preserves are areas having characteristics associated with national parks, but in which Congress has permitted continued public hunting, trapping, oil/gas exploration and extraction. Many existing national preserves, without sport hunting, would qualify for national park designation.

National Historic Sites are sites containing a single historical feature that was directly associated with its subject. Derived from the Historic Sites Act of 1935, a number of historic sites were established by secretaries of the Interior, but most have been authorized by acts of Congress.

National Memorials are sites that are commemorative of a historic person or episode; they need not occupy sites historically connected with their subject.

So there you have it.

According to the legend, you must tread carefully at Pipestone, as the eggs of the Thunderbird are buried there. The Park Service brochure contented itself with a warning to stay on the path "For Your Safety". It was not the last time on my journey that visions of the Yellow Brick Road sprang to mind.

I believe in respecting other people's beliefs. I just don't believe in believing them. I am especially skeptical of ideas couched in terms I consider mythological, such as Great Spirit and Thunderbird.

Recently we have begun to misunderstand the value of culture, intent on preserving it as birthright rather than gift. Culture has value in so far as it provides a path to truth. Culture is least valuable and most dangerous to those who claim possession of it.

But searching for truth is a lot like searching for monuments: you never know what it will look like. My skepticism is exactly balanced by my bewilderment. My motto is: if you're not confused, you don't understand.

The Pipestone brochure contained a map of the monument area. The path in front of me, called the Circle Trail, cut a large amorphous circuit through the woods and grassland. Despite the heat of the day (very warm for September in Minnesota), I ambled through the historic grounds, wandering in and out of shade, staying respectfully on the path. Either the other slide show graduates had gone ahead or they decided to pass on the grounds altogether. I was alone.

A few dozen yards along, a small bridge crossed over a shallow brook. I stood on the bridge, hot, thirsty, bored, disappointed, watching the shallow water trickle by. I was ready to leave.

Then I heard the music.

The percolating noise of the water rippled around me as I stood on the bridge. But the brook was not babbling. It was singing.

Not singing singing. No words. No pop tunes. No Top Forty. The brook made noise like any other brook, water splashing down over the stone stream bed. But somewhere inside the natural pop and bubble was a purity, a color, like no instrument I had ever heard.

I knelt down to listen. It wasn't just the quality of sound that attracted me, but the musicality. There were overtones, timbres, echoes, earthy but not earthly, resonating, connected, not random reverberation but a lattice, evocative, like no tonal hierarchy I knew, with the barest glimpse of architecture, with line and counterpoint, with variations interwoven.

It was as if the stream had composed a symphony.

It was absurd. A stream couldn't make music. Only humans can make music. Yes, I know, I said birds and whales and so forth, song, yes, but not music.

Maybe it was something in the stone, or the way the streambed rested on the compressed layers of quartzite and pipestone, maybe something in the speed of the water, or the mineral content, or the declination of the land.

Or.

Maybe the ground was Sacred. Maybe the Great Spirit had descended from the heavens and consecrated the earth in this place. It didn't seem quite so farfetched then as I knelt close to the stream to listen.

I am a trained musician. I know what I heard.

Go there.

Listen.

Then tell me I'm not crazy.

Please.

I don't know how long I sat there. People passed by. They didn't stop. Maybe they didn't hear the music. Maybe they were afraid of the strange man holding his silver tape recorder down to the stream. I don't know.

Finally I stood. Addled or dazzled, take your pick, I followed the brook uphill and upstream. A dozen paces beyond the bridge, I heard another sound, different but familiar, and one I have always loved.

Around a curve in the path, the brook descended in a waterfall, only three or four feet in height and not much more than that in width. A sign revealed the lilting onomatopoetic name: Winnewissa Falls, from the Dakota language, meaning jealous maiden.

I imagined more than felt the hint of a light cool spray as I listened to Jealous Maiden falls. In the spring with the melting winter snows, the falls would have been boisterous. But it had been a dry summer, and a hushed and tranquil whoosh filled the air.

Again I listened closely. It was only noise, not music. I was relieved actually, thankful that I wasn't going to be hearing celestial music from water fountains and garden hoses. Or mailboxes and parking meters.

The sound of a waterfall is a natural kind of white noise. Rainfall and ocean waves are other examples.

White noise contains equal amounts of sound in every frequency that humans can hear (roughly 20 hertz to 20 kilohertz). It can be generated artificially by feeding a series of random numbers into a digital signal generator. Studies have shown that white noise can induce relaxation, reduce the sensation of pain, and even promote healing.

But the white noise of a waterfall is not really random. The sounds are simply too complex for a human ear to distinguish.

The music in a waterfall, each note separated and played individually in perpendicular time, a five-dimensional version of our four-dimensional music, would require more powerful senses or a higher intelligence to apprehend. What seemed like noise to us could be a cantata for artificial intelligence or alien minds.

In the movie *Contact*, the original alien signal consisted of prime numbers. In the harmonics of the signal, a television picture was encoded. And interlaced within the TV waves was another signal containing instructions for the alien erector set.

Maybe that's why I loved the noise of a waterfall. It only seemed like noise.

Curling up and around Winnewissa Falls, the path led to the upper grassland plain. A small lake had formed at the top, a pond really, maybe fifty yards across, dotted and dashed by small stone islands.

The surface of the pond was unbroken, perfectly still, as though it had fallen asleep. Yet every once in a while, something underneath (a turtle or muskrat?) would rustle the water and concentric ripples would spread throughout the watery plane. Along the shoreline, dragonflies flitted without sound over the reeds. There was no other movement, no breeze even to tease the grasses.

Again there was no music, not even any noise. The place was serene as a church, and silent.

Any musician knows the uses of silence. This noiseless void could have been just a pastoral rest note in a geologic symphony, molto adagio e pianissimo, or maybe even the silence before the score, the Cosmic conductor's baton upraised, or the intake of breath before the macrocosmic chorus. If it lasted a hundred years, or a thousand, or a million, who would know?

Or maybe the music was ultra or subsonic, a Dragonfly Sonata, too high or too low for poor human ears, the way dogs bark and crickets chirp at the low frequency sound waves of an earthquake before anything can be felt by humans.

At the far side of the pond, a wooden marker pointed up stairs roughhewn deep into massive stone. I stepped up onto a broad rock outcropping. At the top, too-bright sunlight flooded a borderless sky.

Across a divide, almost hidden in the trees, a crag formed the outline of an old woman, perhaps the jealous maiden herself in later life, with a pronounced chin, long overhanging nose, shadow eye, and wrinkled cracks in the stone, all framed by green and brown locks of leaves and branches that tumbled down her shoulder. How much had she aged, I wondered, in the hundreds of years that men (by ironic tradition women were not allowed) had been climbing to see her?

Indians had named the formation the Oracle. According to legend, the shaman stood on top of the outcropping and asked the Oracle for guidance. If he were favored, an answer would issue from the craggy stone lips.

I waited.

I had lots of questions.

But I didn't hear any words. I guess I wasn't favored. I certainly wasn't a shaman.

Then something passed very fast over my head.

Two hawks circled each other, swooping and gliding, falling and flying in patterns only they understood. They might have been playing, or courting. Maybe they were dancing. Sunlight shone through luminous wings, angel white against cool cloudless blue.

Rooted to the rock, I was mesmerized by their superhuman grace. But I wanted to join them. I wanted to dance too in that blue-white stream, floating and gliding, drifting, emergent in spins and curves of innate inhuman equation, soaring in circles that made no sense except to the sky.

Without warning, one of the hawks flew off, hurtling west, vanishing into the blinding glare of orange brilliance suspended above the line of trees. The other hawk circled alone.

I turned to go.

Blue sun-yellow sky images danced in my visual field as I climbed carefully down from the rocky platform. Back on the path, I wandered, still blind— the Really Tall Weeds were Really Tall. Treading cautiously to evade a host of green-yellowish grasshoppers marking the way, I finally emerged into the open and found the Visitor Center again.

My vision mostly cleared, I entered the claustrophobic gift shop. Traditional carvings made of pipestone were neatly displayed in glass-top cases. The larger items—ceremonial pipes and other artifacts—decorated the walls.

The pipes themselves, wine-colored stone intricately carved, were too expensive for an unemployed wanderer. But from beneath the glass layer, a menagerie of miniature pipestone totems gazed up at me. Each tiny figurine represented a different animal spirit with its own domain and power.

You might have expected I would choose a hawk. But I was drawn instead to a pipestone turtle about an inch long, a fertility totem of all things. It was an odd choice I guess. But it fit just so in my hand.

Turtle in my pocket, moose at my side, I followed the hawk and headed west.

CHAPTER TWO

The Poet

I didn't want to go back the way I came, so I drove out of Pipestone along Route 30, a shady, rolling two-lane country road. The slow pace gave me time to think, to search for a word to describe my experience at Pipestone.

Exhilarating.

Surprising.

Puzzling.

Curious, in the modern sense of something odd and the archaic sense of something crafted.

Weird, in the modern sense of something supernatural and the archaic sense of something destined.

Lost in weird, pondering curious, I barely noticed as I once more crossed the state line into

South Dakota. A few minutes down the tree-shaded lane, my car topped a small hill then coasted to a stop in the middle of the road.

I had seen buffalo in the movies: My favorite was *Dances with Wolves*, which was filmed in South Dakota. The epic score, the sweeping cinematography, and the compelling story, all orchestrated by the multi-talented Kevin Costner, created a nostalgic paradise out of the harsh realities of 1860s Dakota territory.

Relics of that paradise were now confronting me. Penned tightly in a corral near the road, a small herd of buffalo (or more correctly American bison) stood nearly motionless. Most were oblivious to me (used to being objects of attention I guess), though one seemed to be glaring directly at me. But that was not the most perplexing aspect of the encounter.

The corral backed up against a grain silo, which stood just a few yards from a weathered, well-tended farmhouse. White-curtained windows faced the L-shaped front porch with the sagging roof and wooden swing just big enough for two.

Somehow two distinct and incompatible images had merged in the same canvas, as if Remington had retouched American Gothic or John

Wayne had had ridden into an Andy Hardy feature. Someone had broken our icons and glued the pieces back together none too carefully.

Unable to resolve the incongruities, I accelerated past the puzzle and soon turned south and hit I-90. But if I was hoping to regain familiarity on the interstate, I was disappointed. As I swung past Sioux Falls, the walls of the world dissolved.

There was just—there.

Extent.

Expanse.

My line of sight unbroken to the blurred horizon, I glimpsed the world as the ancients imagined, a circle beneath the domes of heaven. The perspective was unsettling at first, as if I had been indoors all my life and had ventured outside for the first time. Now I was truly on the prairie, not the Euclidean farmland plots of Minnesota, but the vast tundra of the Great Plains. There was nowhere to hide.

The ground around me was flatter than anywhere else I had been, but not perfectly flat as I expected. The plateau rolled, like an ocean of earth, with swells miles long between trough and crest, and tilted in a modified sine wave, the way a sparrow flies, briefly pumping its wings on the upswing, then tucking and coasting on the long downswing. In that motion, quick surge-slow descent, the earth swept imperceptibly, with geologic velocity, toward the invisible mountains of the west.

For hours that day, I ventured up and down the long, long, loooonnnngggggg swells of South Dakota, surfing the waves of turf for several hundred miles, breathing emancipation in with the prairie air. I did nothing, felt no need to do anything, but drive.

The boundless view heightened an exhilaration mounting inside me, propelled by something I barely recognized: freedom. I had lived by schedules for forty years, driven by deadlines in school and work and even theater. But now I was driving, and no one, including me, knew where I was going, or when I would get there. A typical day on my journey consisted of:

Waking when I wanted.

Eating when I wanted.

Driving where I wanted.

Seeing what I wanted.

Stopping when I wanted.

Sleeping when I wanted.

I just followed my instincts and the road in front of me. Leisurely is the word you may be thinking of. Or lazy. But to me, this was Heaven by lack of design, Arcadia of the Indolent. And beneath the freedom, there was something else, barely remembered, yet vaguely familiar: joy.

*
*
*

We know we're awake because our eyes are open.

By late afternoon, I was ready to stretch my legs. Following a particularly long swell of highway, I reached the top of a bluff. Spotting a rest stop across the highway, I pulled across and into the parking lot.

Set back a few hundred yards from the edge of the bluff, the building was long and low, mostly one big room, with a massive rectangular information desk in the center manned by several busy aides. Beneath the windows, low slung metal racks brimmed with brochures describing every attraction you could imagine, and many you couldn't.

I strolled outside the building towards the bluff. The grass was tall, not Really Tall, but enough to hide a snake or two. So I kept my head down heading toward the brink. At the edge of the bluff, I looked up.

The slope fell sharply away hundreds of yards to where the Missouri River engraved a broad S through the grasslands. Beyond the wide impassive river, the brown flat earth stretched to the curve of the world, melding into a white horizon unguessably distant. But it wasn't the distance that held me to the spot.

There are qualities that belong to a place, that inhabit its essence and mark it in the memory. The quality of this bluff was Blue.

Blue has many names: azure, sapphire, navy, even cornflower. I have never seen a cornflower, or any blue flower for that matter. But cornflower blue I can picture in my mind: draw a luster from the earth, blend in sunlight, sift in moonlight.

What I saw from the bluff was not any blue I could imagine: not azure nor sapphire nor navy nor cornflower. Even now, when I close my eyes, I can't picture it. But I can remember how it felt, dodging my eyes and seeping unfiltered through the pores of my skin: Blueness, essence of Blue, narcotic Blue. Manifest Blue. True Blue. Transcendental Blue.

But there were two blues, not one.

We see the sky as blue because the blue electromagnetic waves of sunlight are shorter and are scattered more easily by the dust in the atmosphere. But nothing about this blue seemed scattered nor did sunlight seem required. Standing there, I realized that I had never truly seen a blue sky before. A stain had been washed from the stratosphere. Blue shone through.

Bodies of water are blue when they reflect the sky. But the Missouri had a different recipe that day, independent of the firmament above. Take a sea, fold it over and over and over like a translucent sheet, then glaze it in a tawny bed of grass. That is Missouri Blue.

Go to the Missouri River crossing.

Stand on the bluff on a cloudless day.

Blue lives there.

*
*
*

Across the blue river, under the blue sky, I passed the night in the town of Chamberlain on the far bank of the Missouri. That night I happily returned to Emerson's *Essays*. After once more browsing the volume, I began reading *The Poet*.

As with *Self-Reliance*, Emerson starts out *The Poet* with some poetry of his own.

> *"A moody child and wildly wise*
> *Pursued the game with joyful eyes,*
> *Which chose, like meteors, their way,*
> *And rived the dark with private ray:"*

In addition to his lectures and essays, Emerson was well-known as a poet, and published many in his lifetime, often in *The Dial*, the magazine he founded (and briefly edited) with his transcendentalist friends and fellows. His most famous poem was probably *The Concord Hymn*, which celebrated the defense of Concord during the Revolutionary War and originated the famous phrase;

> *"Here once the embattled farmers stood,*
> *And fired the shot heard round the world."*

Brahma, published in the Atlantic Monthly in 1857, reflects Emerson's interest in sacred Hindu texts, including the *Bhagavad-Gita*.

"If the red slayer think he slays,
  Or if the slain think he is slain,
They know not well the subtle ways
  I keep, and pass, and turn again.
Far or forgot to me is near,
  Shadow and sunlight are the same,
The vanished gods to me appear,
  And one to me are shame and fame.
They reckon ill who leave me out;
  When me they fly, I am the wings;
I am the doubter and the doubt,
  And I the hymn the Brahmin sings.
The strong gods pine for my abode,
  And pine in vain the sacred Seven;
But thou, meek lover of the good!
  Find me, and turn thy back on heaven."

My personal favorite of Emerson's poems is entitled *Give All to Love*. The sentimental title contradicts the final steely prescription:

"Though thou loved her as thyself,
As a self of purer clay,
Though her parting dims the day,
Stealing grace from all alive;
Heartily know,
When half-gods go,
The gods arrive."

STEPHEN EVANS

When I first started reading Emerson's poetry, I thought it well-crafted but, with a few exceptions (*Terminus*, for example, which could have been written by Yeats), generally lacking the power of his prose. But he was a great promoter of other poets, including Henry Thoreau and Jones Very. His famous letter to Walt Whitman on *Leaves of Grass* congratulated the younger poet at the beginning of a great career. Whitman included the letter in subsequent editions, and had it published in the New York Tribune.

Emerson's primary influence on poetry comes not from his own verse, or even his encouragement and praise of other poets, but from his idea what a poet should be. In the essay, he starts out drawing a distinction between those who write poetry and those who are poets.

> *"For it is not metres, but a metre-making argument, that makes a poem,--a thought so passionate and alive, that, like the spirit of a plant or an animal, it has architecture of its own, and adorns nature with a new thing."*

Emerson was not preaching revolution in poetry, but invoking a cosmology of truth. And at the center he places not the man of religion or the man of science, but the man of words: the poet. The greatest American practitioner of the art lived not far from Emerson, even heard him lecture in her home town of Amherst, Massachusetts. Born in 1830, Emily Dickinson was twelve when Emerson wrote:

"the world seems always waiting for its poet."

Reading *The Poet* that night, I was not swept away by the language, as I had been the night before with *Self-Reliance* But his language heightens at the end of the essay, where he breathlessly lays out the path of the poet.

"The world is full of renunciations and apprenticeships, and this is thine: thou must pass for a fool and a churl for a long season...Thou shalt have the whole land for thy park and manor, the sea for thy bath and navigation, without tax and without envy; the woods and the rivers thou shalt own; and thou shalt possess that wherein others are only tenants and boarders. Thou true land-lord! sea-lord! air-lord! Wherever snow falls, or water flows, or birds fly, wherever day and night meet in twilight, wherever the blue heaven is hung by clouds, or sown with stars, wherever are forms with transparent boundaries, wherever are outlets into celestial space, wherever is danger,

and awe, and love, there is Beauty, plenteous as rain, shed for thee, and though thou shouldest walk the world over, thou shalt not be able to find a condition inopportune or ignoble."

The next morning, I considered following the Missouri River north toward Pierre. But I decided instead to stick with I-90. So far it had not disappointed me.

West of the Missouri, the world moved by faster and I began to think in time instead of miles. A few hours down the road, just west of Murdo, South Dakota, I came across what looked like a movie set nearly concealed behind a tall uneven wood fence. Alert by then to hidden oddities, I pulled off the highway to investigate.

The fences converged around an old barn with a couple of gas pumps out front. The sign said 1880 Town. I had no idea what that meant.

Just inside the door, I paid the $6 entrance fee to a man crouched behind a booth, who said nothing but passed me a brochure (apparently the principle method of communication thereabouts), and motioned toward some heavy curtains across a doorway. I passed through the curtains, half-expecting to find a sign pointing to the Egress, the P. T. Barnum version of crowd control at his Museum of American Oddities in New York.

Instead, I found the Wild West version of Barnum's museum. The rustic room was large and square, with unpainted walls and unfinished wooden floors. Saddles and holsters and lariats hung from aging rafters, along with other worn and weathered items that I could not identify. Beneath the dangled vestiges of history, a miniature maze of counters topped with smudgy glass revealed a chaotic collection of old bottles, straight razors, tin badges.

The sawdusty floorboards creaked as I strolled from showcase to showcase, wondering who had owned each item, how was it lost, how found, how longed for. How many forgotten stories would never be told? Lifetimes worth, in that one room.

The second floor of the barn was completely different. Unlike the jumble of the lower floor, the upper floor was a museum for the film *Dances with Wolves*. Sets and props used in filming had been painstakingly arranged in a series of dioramas, each one depicting a scene. The largest display showed a Civil War surgical tent and medical implements. In the movie, Kevin Costner, playing Union Lieutenant John Dunbar, escapes from the medical tent, steals a horse, and gallops along Confederate lines in a suicide attempt that spurs his Union compatriots.

Walking through that building was like traveling through a mind, not the ganglia and neurons of a brain but the virtual aggregation of mentality: the creaky barn the persona; the silent clerk the sensory gatekeeper; the lower floor the random hodgepodge, bits and bytes, of memory. The top floor transformed these elements into the recollections, the crafted ceremony of the stories we tell ourselves about who we are. Invisible all around was the organizing homunculus: the transcendental Director.

After Dancing with Wolves for a while on the second floor, I drifted down the stairs, egressed out the back of the barn, and emerged from one movie set into another, much larger one.

In the musical *Brigadoon*, a century-old town appears from the mists of the Scottish highlands. Here in South Dakota was an Old West Brigadoon, an entire town transported through time from the western frontier. But these were no false-front set pieces. Real buildings had been rescued from demolition, transported to the site, and painstaking arranged to recreate our entertainment-enhanced preconceptions of the American West. If the barn was the mind, the memories and the recollections, the town itself was the memoir—the perfected ejected fantasy.

Like a typical Western movie set, the town had been laid out with the buildings placed on either side of a Main Street several hundred feet long. Randolph Scott would have been much obliged to tread the wooden boardwalks that lined each side of the street. I would have too, but I lacked the boots and spurs to produce the proper clomp and jingle.

The interior of each structure had been faithfully renovated, and fully outfitted with antique furniture and trappings. Every category of mythic Western edifice was in evidence: the barbershop (and bath), the saloon, the Marshall's office, the bank, the newspaper, the general store, and more. There was even a little white church at the High Noon end of the street. It was perfect. I couldn't help admiring the imagination of the proprietors in saving these wonderful old buildings and making them useful and beautiful again.

At the opposite end of the street from the church, I found a livery stable, historically outfitted like the rest of the town, but not so artfully arranged. This gear looked like it was actually being used. Then I saw why. A paddock at the side of the stable held one other attraction: Cisco.

Cisco was Kevin Costner's horse in *Dances with Wolves*. The animal (whose non-stage name was Buck) had also been transported to the town. But he did not look happy about it. Head down, he never moved but for a sporadic listless swish of his tail. Cisco looked really depressed.

It was understandable, really; it must have been traumatic to go from movie star to roadside attraction. Did he miss the lights? The stars? The hay flown in especially for him?

I wondered if Kevin Costner knew about Cisco. What horse was Costner riding now? Did he love that horse? Were they planning colts? It occurred to me that my personal history might be influencing my reaction to Cisco's plight.

Still. Something had to be done. I could save Cisco. I could leap on his back, jump him over the fence, and ride madly to Canada and freedom. That's what Kevin Costner would have done.

I looked in Cisco's eyes. It wasn't me he wanted. There was no answer to that.

I left Cisco to his memories.

And me to mine.

*
*

*

The route to Badlands National Park is a horseshoe-shaped road called the Loop, which starts on I-90, extends through Buffalo Gap National Grasslands until it reaches the park, then swings back around until it hits I-90 again at the town of Wall, South Dakota.

Just off I-90 on the Loop, I stopped to get a Coke at a small establishment that reminded me of a tiny shop near my former home in Minneapolis. The Loop store didn't have SUPERSIZE cokes. But they did have bags of unsalted peanuts to feed to the prairie dogs who lived next door.

I have a great fondness for anything squirrelly (Class Mammalia Order Rodentia I mean). I think my infatuation began with Freddy, a grey squirrel who moved in next door in Minneapolis.

In Minneapolis, we lived in the top two floors of a Victorian house only two blocks from Lake of the Isles. The lake was known for, well, isles of course—two of them near the northwest lakeshore—but also for its wildlife.

In the winter, around the south side of the lake, you could sometimes catch sight of the rare Snow Serpent, a Norse American cousin of the Loch Ness Monster who hibernated in summer and prowled the icy lake in winter. Many a snowman has been devoured by this sly leviathan.

In the spring, an armada of Canadian geese invaded the lake. Each evening, the royal navy embarked from the lakeshore to their island harbor, a squadron of goslings in regal tow. On the island closest to land, a small sign stood akilter, nearly covered by the tall grasses. The sign read Game Preserve in wavering letters that might have been painted by webbed feet.

About two blocks up from the western shore, there was a tiny shop/grocery store/cafe that couldn't decide what it wanted to be when it grew up. We often stopped to get ice cream and cappuccino in summer or cappuccino and ice cream in winter. Lake of the Isles was the apex of nature for me: serenity plus espresso.

Two separate paths circumnavigated the lakes of Minneapolis. The outer path was for Speeders: bikers and inline skaters and other mobility enthusiasts. While I admired their dexterity, balance, and tight clothing, I always thought it was odd to be in such a hurry when you're moving in a circle.

The inner path around the lakes was for Footers: joggers, walkers, and plodders like me. The inner path was often flooded during the spring thaw, forcing both Footers and Speeders onto the same ground, a recipe for disaster. There was just no getting around me.

On the first floor of our house (or the second or third floor, depending on where you started counting), the guest bedroom looked out over a large square white-washed deck that was built on top of the garage. Between the deck and the neighbor's yard grew a slim tree, tall and straight with no branches for at least thirty feet.

About twenty feet up the trunk, someone had fixed a homemade birdhouse. It was there when we moved in, and, given the weathered exterior, possibly many years before, though it doesn't take long to look weathered in Minnesota.

The birdhouse was maybe eight inches wide and about a foot tall to the top of the arched roof. A hole an inch or so wide opened in front, enough to accommodate a finch or wren. From the guestroom window, you could look directly at and into the birdhouse.

When we moved in, the birdhouse was empty. In fact, we never saw a bird express the least interest, maybe because the neighbor's tiny dog was constantly barking up the tree to roust any potential occupants.

A white picket fence three feet high separated our backyard from the neighbor's. The barrier was patrolled at various times during the day by a terrier with curly black hair who yapped without provocation (that I could see) or relief (that I could hear).

Day after day as I sat in my office and pretended to write, the obnoxious yelping continued, until finally one day I stormed down the front steps, out the door, up and over the deck, to confront the little monster.

I don't know what I planned to do.

Maybe bark back.

The dog continued to yowl ferociously until I was about ten feet away. Then he spotted me stomping furiously toward him.

In an instant, the little guy was transformed. He stopped barking, and his stubby tail wagged faster than the flight of the bumblebee as he launched himself in delight, up and down, back and forth, over and over, all along the fence.

Embarrassed at my irritation, I reached over to pet him. Which was hard, because he kept trying to jump up and lick my hand.

Maybe he barked because it was his job.

Maybe he was lonely.

Maybe he just wanted to meet the new neighbors.

He didn't stop barking after that day. But from then on, whenever I heard him, I had to smile at the memory of his conversion, and mine.

I often wondered why the local bats didn't take up residence in the birdhouse. In fact, I hoped they would, but I guess they preferred our bedroom (a converted attic), since we occasionally awoke to find one circling over our bed. I may praise the ecological benefits of certain rodents, flying and otherwise, but I don't recommend them as roommates.

One day, after about a year of vacancy, I leaned out of the guestroom window to find a squirrel similarly poking his head out of the birdhouse door. We immediately named him Freddy. I don't know why.

I began feeding Freddy and his brethren and sistern, depositing hulled sunflower seed along the banister of the deck. This practice made us hugely popular with the local inhabitants.

One squirrel, a neighbor from across the street, waited each morning for me to leave the house. This was his cue to hop delicately across the telephone line over the street, flop onto the neighbor's house, plop onto their tree, then drop down to our deck to munch. We called him Mopsy.

Freddy became a very popular squirrel in the neighborhood, what with having a spiffy house and trained humans at his beck and call. So he soon enraptured a lovely female, whom with some political incorrectness we named Mrs. Freddy, and then two tiny heads poked out of the small round doorway as we scurried for the camera.

Often we would see Freddy sprawled out over the roof of the house enjoying whatever sunlight was available. I imagined that this was when Mrs. Freddy was vacuuming, or possibly vice versa.

Carpenter work soon began on the birdhouse. Little by little Freddy gnawed the door wider to accommodate the new occupant. We once saw three grey heads poking out, but we never learned whether the third was an interloper or a visiting cousin from Duluth.

In the oddly intimate springtime interlude after my wife and I decided to separate but before I actually left Minnesota, I was sitting in my office when I heard a fierce chittering noise. I looked outside to see another squirrel pursuing Mrs. Freddy with extramarital intentions.

Freddy chased the other squirrel, who chased Mrs. Freddy, down his tree, across the deck, and up another tall tree next to the sidewalk out front. The adversaries raced one another around and around the tree until Freddy was cornered far out on a slim branch. The other squirrel charged out, the branch bowed under the weight, and Freddy plunged thirty feet in a dead fall directly onto the sidewalk.

Even through the closed front window, the sickening smack of his tiny body hitting the concrete horrified me. Sure he was dead, I started to run down to the rescue. Again, I don't know what I planned to do, though massaging his little chest and shouting Clear! did jump to mind.

But miraculously, Freddy rose, gingerly testing himself with a few unsteady steps, stunned, yet still able to walk. But the fight was over. The other squirrel had won. Freddy clambered back to his tree house, dazed and alone.

I never saw any more visitors to Freddy's house. Mrs. Freddy never returned. I would often see Freddy by himself, his head dangling out the now too wide door. I'm not sure he knew what happened to him. But at least he got the house.

Anthropomorphosis means to attribute human characteristics to nonhuman entities. An alternate meaning is the transformation into human form. The word is derived from two ancient Greek words—anthropos, which means human, and morphe, which means form. Morpheus (in Greek mythology, not the modern myth of The Matrix) was the god of dreams, and could take any human form.

In our common discourse, we are often naturally anthropomorphic, speaking of inanimate objects as if they were sentient. The computer won't talk to the printer. The battery is dead. Sometimes we even speak to them, cajoling or cursing as the moment requires.

The more complex the behavior, the more we rely on the language of intelligence to describe the action. You could if you like extend this observation into a linguistic demonstration of God's existence, much like medieval scholars Anselm and Aquinas did with their obscure ontological proofs (ontology is the study of the way things are).

The proof would go like this: If a description of complex action requires reference to intelligence, then a description of the most complex action—the creation and ordering of the universe—

must require reference to the greatest intelligence: God, or what you will.

In a blasphemous reverse anthropomorphosis, we historically attribute human emotions to God. The *Old Testament* is full of the God of Wrath and Vengeance. The *New Testament* speaks of the God of Love and Mercy. But the supreme intelligence and creator of this incomprehensibly vast and complex cosmos is far less likely to have human feelings than a squirrel.

I've tried without much success to imagine a nonhuman mind; consciousness without language eludes me. Does a dog dream of a man the way a man dreams of a dog? But imagining that animals have human feelings is more truthful than imagining they don't.

I am an inveterate anthropomorphizer, I know, constantly attributing human feelings to nonhuman and even nonanimate beings. But that's not an accident. For me, anthropomorphosis is a lifestyle choice, a path to understanding, a methodology of truth—or as close as we can get to it today.

Prairie dogs are related to squirrels, but I had never seen a real one before. So I looped out of the Loop store with a meager twelve ounce can of Coke in one hand and a bag of unsalted peanuts in the other.

Next to the store, an area maybe fifty feet wide and twice that long had been fenced off. Within the enclosure, little mounds dotted the ground, spaced out about ten feet from one another, with a hole in the top. In most of the holes, a lone prairie dog was ensconced, noggin and paws just visible above the ground. I thought of Freddy immediately.

Other prairie dogs were waddle-scrambling around the enclosure, trying to look cute enough to coax a peanut out of an easy mark tourist like me. Most of them were well fed, so I guess they were good at their jobs.

For a century or more, prairie dogs have been wrongly considered the scourge of the Western grasslands. Ranchers have accused them of destroying the grazing lands used by cattle, and found their holes dangerous going for horses. Prairie dogs have been hunted, exterminated by poison gas, even suffocated by having their communities bulldozed. They are in fact an endangered species, though politics and potential litigation have stalled the official designation.

Fortunately, and hopefully in time, ecologists are now correcting the erroneous beliefs about prairie dogs. Prairie dogs are beneficial to the grasslands and many species in the prairie ecosystem depend on them in one way or another.

I was doing my part to save the prairie dog, spreading my peanuts around like birdseed, when I noticed one sitting in his hole. He looked directly at me, but didn't approach like the others to get a peanut. I immediately named him Lloyd. Again I'm not sure why, except that I didn't know anyone named Lloyd, so the name was available.

Lloyd was obviously the veteran of the group. One ear was notched, and the bare spot on his head didn't look like male pattern baldness. He was maybe twenty feet from me, a long toss for a peanut. Nevertheless, I made the attempt and the peanut landed about a foot away, a decent throw I thought. But Lloyd was not impressed and didn't budge from his hole. Another prairie dog ran over and quickly nabbed Lloyd's peanut.

I tried again, landing the next peanut maybe six inches from the hole. Again Lloyd didn't stir. Again another prairie dog robbed Lloyd of his rightful due.

I lobbed another, not as close. By this time, the other prairie dogs were beginning to get the idea and were clustering around Lloyd waiting for offerings.

I held the next peanut in my hand as though it were a tiny basketball. I was once a pretty fair basketball player. After I gave up my opera career, I considered turning pro, limited only by the fact that I was short, slow, and couldn't jump. I could shoot though.

I lifted my hands over my head and tried my jump shot, which is different from most jump shots in that my feet never leave the ground. The peanut rose about fifteen feet in the air, descended gracefully, and hit Lloyd smack on the head. Then it bounced a few inches outside the rim of the hole.

If someone hit me on the head with a peanut, I would react. Lloyd never flinched. He simply glared at me as though I were crazy. But I noticed that none of the other prairie dogs moved in to get this peanut.

Lloyd knew what he wanted, and what he didn't. Clearly he didn't want my peanuts.

I began to wonder whether it was everyone's peanuts, or just my peanuts he didn't crave. Maybe he was on duty, like the guards at Buckingham Palace or the castle of the Wicked Witch of the West. Maybe he just didn't want me to see him eat the peanut, wouldn't give me the satisfaction. Maybe he was too proud for peanuts, remembering the old days when his father took him hunting for Really Tall Weeds like his father before him and his father before him.

It's a mystery.

But if someone doesn't want your peanuts, don't drive yourself nuts wondering why. No sense breaking your heart over peanuts.

*
*
*

I rapidly disbursed the rest of my peanuts to the waiting prairie dogs and proceeded down the Loop toward the Badlands. Far down the road (and I could see far down the road), there was a tiny oblong structure in the middle of the highway. At first it looked as if someone had constructed a phone booth in the median. But as I got closer, I realized the building was a toll booth.

The little booth stood alone, completely isolated and the only thing taller than the tall grass across miles and miles of treeless prairie, as if some enterprising soul had erected a booth at a random spot and was charging a toll to Nowhere.

As I approached, I surrendered to the surreality and obediently paid the entry fee (six dollars again, though I was half-expecting it to be a gold coin from under my tongue).

Beyond the booth, the wind picked up from the west and a ghostly horde of tumbleweeds swarmed over the rise. Fortunately, my sturdy Cavalier was able to fend off the rolling phantoms until I arrived safely at the so-called developed area of Badlands National Park.

If you find an old guidebook, you can still see the park referred to as Badlands National Monument, since that's how the area was first designated in 1939. In 1978, the area was redesignated a National Park, for which I was extremely grateful. I don't always learn a lesson the first time around and searching for monuments in the Badlands would have been a challenge. The park covers almost 250,000 acres in southwestern South Dakota, over 64,000 acres of which are designated as Wilderness area. Only a small area of the park along the Loop is developed, which in Badlands parlance means someone stopped there once.

Farther along, the Loop began to actually loop, curving around to the west, until a solitary parking lot came into view. A ridge about fifteen feet high blocked the view to the south. In every other direction, only scrub brush and bare rock were visible. I had paid the toll to Nowhere. Now here was the parking lot. I pulled in, figuring I might as well get my money's worth.

Along the base of the ridge ran a concrete path called the Notch Trail, a name not especially comforting, recalling as it did images of gunfighters and Colt 45s. I walked warily, hoping that Nowhere would eventually lead Somewhere.

Not far down the trail, the ridge dipped sharply for a few feet (oh, that kind of notch). As I stepped up into the opening, the parched earth slipped away under my feet. Struggling to find a foothold, I leaned far out through the V-shaped opening.

A number of times on my journey, I was misled by names. The Plains weren't plain. The Black Hills were green. I won't even start about Devil's Tower, except to say that it wasn't. I saw no yellow in Yellowstone. Language is instinctive in humans. Linguistic patterns are genetic in origin, just like the ability to distinguish shape and color. DNA can be considered a language of sorts (which I suppose makes sex a conversation).

Names are all too human, an inborn efficiency of our species, a function, a power. We impose our nominal fashions on the universe to dress it according to our needs, tools of thought and survival and naturally selective expedience. These names strangle our understanding, twisting our impressions into form-fitting packages.

Names represent classes, congregations, groups. Yet a name is a distinction, a methodology of simplification, of inclusion and exclusion. But in a search for a common identity, we sacrifice individuality. It's a poor exchange. Rose is not a rose, nor is a rose a rose.

Names point to facts. Facts are seductive. Names are seductive. Distinctions, though occasionally factual, are inherently not True. In all the universe there is only One and All.

Symbols are the opposite of names. Names are walls. Symbols are doorways. As a child I watched an eclipse by punching a hole in cardboard and observing the solar projection. Symbols are like that, the earthbound projection of a celestial event blazing through a slit onto the palm of a hand, the visible glimmer of the fireball.

Today we have lost the knack for symbols. Their power has gone missing, faded to names, phantoms not flares. The mass of us lead desperate lives of quiet abstraction.

The name Badlands refers to an arid area that exhibits high rates of erosion. Nothing in the name prepares you for the view.

Five million years ago, the same geological forces that created the Rocky Mountains also raised part of the broad MidAmerican plain. The White river, which now flows miles away from the park, eroded the rock and volcanic ash that make up the plain, carving over eons a cliff.

Even now the exposed face of the upper plain, called the Wall, continues to erode about one inch per year. Of varying height, the Wall is a hundred miles of broken surface that exposes layer on geological layer of soil and rock and compacted volcanic ash, each layer three or four feet high and marked by distinct color changes.

That is the geology. The phenomenology is harder to explain.

We never knew the wasteland would be beautiful.

Beyond the ridgeline where I stood, the land fell away steeply, plunging in a sharp decline a hundred feet, then opening into a blasted plain that stretched to the horizon unbroken and untouched. Scattered stunted trees and accumulations of brush dotted the expanse, lush by comparison with the barren Wall itself.

Close by, the terrain was arid, harsh, and stunning. Uncanny spires in bizarre shapes, some hundreds of feet tall, loomed over the desert landscape. Eerie errant minarets stood isolated by time in space, as eon by eon the wall dissolved around them, chiseled by the careless caress of wind and water.

Even more bizarre, along the face of the escarpment below me, row on row of tinted strata cascaded down the slope in endless bands of pale yellow, faint rose, ash grey, waves of pastel Op Art patterns traversing the length of the wall like ribbons, like a mountainous layer cake or gargantuan candy cane, disappearing around curves and promontories, only to reappear farther on. Gazing down from the heights, I had a god's-eye view of the color-coded rocks of ages.

I fumbled through my knapsack and found my cell phone, desperate to share the experience. But there was no service. It was the only place on my trip that my cell phone didn't work. Maybe that's the modern definition of Badlands.

After a long period in silence, I scrambled back down the ridge, the dusty soil crumbling under my feet, and walked silently back to my car.

Continuing my loop around the Loop, I encountered the Fossil Exhibit trail. I have loved paleontology since I was a child, having spent many happy hours in the Dinosaur Hall at the Smithsonian. I knew that the Badlands were a bountiful source of fossils from many eras, but especially the Oligocene epoch. During this a post-dinosaur age beginning some thirty million years ago, mammoths, saber-tooth cats, and the ancestors of the horse and rhinoceros ruled the landscape until humans arrived some twenty thousand years ago or so. But on this quarter-mile trail, the 'fossils' consisted of a few plaster-like casts covered in plastic. After such otherworldly spectacle, the trail was underwhelming and I quickly moved on.

The road curved more sharply around and down the Wall and onto the lower plain. At the bottom of the escarpment, I arrived at the inevitable visitors center, where I was just in time for a film (no slide show this time). The slick production presented the history of the Badlands and various attractions of the park. Beside the theater, a small museum exhibited common Badlands flora and fauna.

Not far from the visitors center was Cedar Pass Lodge, the only accommodations in the park other than campgrounds. Under a contract with the Park Service, the lodge was run by the Oglala tribe of the Lakota nation. The rustic main building held a dining room and gift shop. Twenty or so tiny cabins housed guests nearby.

I desperately wanted to stay in one of the cabins. I had visions of myself the following day: amateur paleontologist hiking boldly into the wilderness to hunt saber-tooth and mastodon fossils, most likely finding rabbits and rattlers (actually, removing fossils from any national park is illegal).

Each year, Badlands park rangers have to rescue a number of unwary or unlucky travelers. Probably I would have swelled their number that year by one clueless wanderer.

Fortunately, I was saved from such foolhardiness; no cabins were available that night. I did get a reservation for the following night, thanks to my whining to the charming desk clerk. (During my trip, I seldom spoke to anyone but desk clerks, tour guides, and fast food cashiers.)

Since there were still a few hours before sunset, I drove back along the Loop to the nearest of the Badlands trails. The steps of the Cliff Shelf Nature trail ran in a circle a few hundred yards long, down the slope of the Wall and back up again.

By the time I reached the bottom, beads of sweat had pooled on my brow; there were a lot of steps and it was desert hot. The stair flattened out into a boardwalk that circled a grove of juniper trees, and a nearby sign explained that the temperature inside the juniper grove was a few degrees cooler than where I was. Not being one to turn down any measure of comfort on a searing (and Cokeless) day, I squeezed my way through the close-set trunks and entered the heart of the grove.

The temperature difference was small but noticeable, like standing in front of an open refrigerator door (something I do habitually as a kind of grace). As a kid, I had many secret hideouts, usually castles constructed from refrigerator boxes that my father brought home from his store. With much the same feeling of secure solitude, I rested for a while on a log inside the stand of junipers. Occasionally other tourists ambled along the trail. No one else ventured inside the grove.

A splash of red caught my eye. As I moved to investigate, I tried to recall whether the museum had displayed any bright red rattlesnakes.

Shielded under a low-hanging cluster of juniper branches and nearly hidden in tall grass, a flower about a foot high bore a single stunning cylindrical bloom with a color between fire and blood. The triangular petals were shaped like a lotus, but folded like a Grecian urn. Against the dark green of the juniper and the scorched greyish tan of the earth, the red beacon flared in the sunlight.

Delighted to find the bloom hidden in brush hidden in juniper hidden in Nowhere, I took a photo so I would remember. Now I've forgotten the photo, but the memory is clear. I don't know the name of the flower. Yet, if I knew the name, would the flower would remain so clear in my memory?

I kept thinking of the line from *Elegy in a Country Churchyard* by Thomas Gray (as quoted in *Bull Durham*, my favorite baseball movie, also starring Kevin Costner):

> *"Full many a flower is born to blush unseen,*
> *And waste its sweetness on the desert air."*

Emerson, in his poem *The Rhodora*, offers a similar if slightly more encouraging message:

> *"Rhodora! if the sages ask thee why*
> *This charm is wasted on the earth and sky,*
> *Tell them, dear, that, if eyes were made for*

seeing,
Then beauty is its own excuse for Being;
Why thou wert there, O rival of the rose!
I never thought to ask; I never knew;
But in my simple ignorance suppose
The self-same power that brought me there, brought you."

In the oval heart of the grove, crisp juniper breath wiped the sweat from my brow. Surrounded in cool green, red beacon blazing, I sat in lotus position and admired the desert flower and inhaled the chill juniper air and imagined poetry and deserts and flowers and baseball until I stood, collected the sweetness, and walked up the trail.

It was just as many steps up as it was down.

STEPHEN EVANS

CHAPTER THREE

Experience

After I left Badlands National Park, I continued looping until I reached I-90 again at the town of Wall. It was nearly 6:00 PM and a day of climbing escarpments and contemplating flowers had exhausted me. When I saw storm clouds filling the western horizon (how far away I couldn't tell; the land was so flat that judging distance was difficult), I proceeded into Wall to find a place to stay.

Not having a daily plan or agenda had a downside: I never had reservations to stay anywhere. And since I was not the type to throw a sleeping bag out on the roadside, especially one I didn't have, I generally stopped early each day and began a search for shelter.

The franchising of America does have this benefit: decent accommodations were nearly always available, usually at a chain motel near the highway. The only time I was ever turned away was in Deadwood on a Saturday night. But often my lodgings were less than exciting.

There were several motels in Wall, and the one I settled on was both more expensive and more depressing than my usual berth. But I was tired so I didn't complain. A few hours after check-in, the towering black clouds on the horizon finally arrived in the form of a mild shower. I took a nighttime stroll in the warm drizzle, as much to get out of the room as anything else.

In the morning, I had breakfast at a coffee shop nearby and prepared to resume my journey. But not before I visited South Dakota's most famous pharmaceutical establishment. A few blocks into town, I soon found Main Street, and Wall Drug.

The original Wall Drug was a depression-era shop that thrived by enticing highway travelers with free cold water, which I'm sure in those days was quite a treat. And still, all along I-90 in South Dakota, billboard after billboard proclaimed Wall Drug a wonderland.

As I walked in the building, I could see that the quaint monument to 1930s marketing had mushroomed into a vast tourist extravaganza. I strolled the labyrinthine aisles a short while, but after the unearthly (or ultra-earthly) sublimity of the badlands, maybe the contrast was too extreme. I put a mental checkmark by Wall, cancelled my reservation at Cedar Pass Lodge, and continued west.

During the Black Hills gold rush, someone discovered that selling equipment to prospectors was often more profitable than prospecting itself. Rapid City resulted. I arrived in Rapid City around 2:00 P.M. The black cloud of high Plains and low Walls still had me in its grip, so further adventuring was put off for the day. I found a motel just off the highway and checked in.

The gregarious desk attendant noticed my Maryland driver's license and began to tell me how she had lived near Baltimore for a while with her cousin who was married to...that's all I remember. I just smiled and listened. My first extended human contact since leaving Minnesota was exactly what I needed.

I thought seriously about asking her to dinner. But instead, I went searching for an auto supply house.

If the priorities inherent in that decision confuse you, you are not alone. But nothing makes me feel more helpless than car trouble. For some reason, I didn't take that into account before I set out driving alone across America. If I had, I might be writing about Amtrak.

Ever since Ohio (or possibly 1996), my car had been slowly leaking radiator fluid. Periodically, the engine temperature would climb toward the red zone, which made my blood pressure climb toward the red zone. Every few hundred miles I added alternating gallons of water and antifreeze (one of the few operations I could successfully perform on a car).

Finally, outside Columbus, I peeked under the hood long enough to spot a pinhole leak in the radiator hose. Buying a spare hose seemed like a sensible plan. And it only took me five states to think of it.

By the time I found an auto parts store, bought a backup hose, and returned to the motel, the pretty desk attendant was gone. Her replacement lacked both the requisite appeal and gender and had probably never been to Maryland. Unrequited, I stopped by the vending area in the motel and bought a Coke (20 oz.).

Opposite the snack machines, I found a small rack of brochures. Brochure racks offer an irreplaceable public service that, with the advent of the Internet, is surely endangered. Let us unite in protesting the loss of this universally useful resource. We need all the guides we can get.

I harvested a handful of brochures and returned to my room. In page after four-color page, I began to get a vibrant if somewhat disjointed sense of the spirit of the region. Mount Rushmore is the most famous attraction in the Black Hills, but it is hardly the only one. Casinos, museums, national parks, hot springs, and private zoos can all be found within a comfortable distance of Rapid City.

The Black Hills (Paha Sapa in the mellifluous Lakota language) are named for the forests of pine that cover the mountains. From a distance, these pine woods made the mountains look black. Actually, they didn't look black to me from any distance, but we've already covered the nominalist deficiencies of the pioneers.

The pine forests of the Black Hills had a different feel than the predominantly deciduous forests of my home in Maryland. The sparse evergreen groves felt less lush and primordial, more pristine, silent, serene. The difference between deciduous trees (which lose their leaves in autumn) and evergreen trees (which don't) is like the difference between Western and Eastern thought. Whoever finds a deciduous evergreen will discover the Tree of Life.

As will become increasingly obvious through the rest of this book, I have acrophobia: fear of heights. But I was at ease driving through the Black Hills, which are called hills even though they are higher than the hills we call mountains in Maryland.

Nothing in the Black Hills felt precipicy. The ground was solid, durable, except where horns of granite thrust out, escaping from the Underground. Maybe they didn't like caves either.

As it turns out, the Black Hills are full of holes. And I don't mean the ones the miners dug, though there are plenty of those too. In the southernmost end, there is Wind Cave National Park, one of the longest caves in the world, with recorded winds of up to 75 miles per hour. In the middle, you can visit Jewel Cave National Monument, even longer than Wind Cave, and sparkling with calcite ornamentation. But I decided to visit Rushmore Cave, the nearest to Mount Rushmore, or more correctly, just beneath it. So in the morning, before ascending, I descended.

Rushmore Cave is a privately-owned and operated attraction at the foot of Mount Rushmore. A steep bank of steps leads from the parking lot about fifty feet up the mountainside to the gift shop, where I of course bought a Coke (12 oz.) and waited for the next tour.

Fifteen minutes and an empty can later, our intrepid group assembled before our guide to the underworld. She was twenty years old maybe, young, slender, and athletic, yet with the hardened confidence of an experienced wayfarer in the abyss.

At the back of the shop, we passed through a curtain into a narrow tunnel. The cave is actually underneath the mountain, and to get there you have to pass through a tunnel carved through four hundred feet of solid rock, which explains why it was just tall and wide enough for one person at a time. I was in the middle of our little group. A girl about twelve years old walked in front of me and I could hear someone behind me. I don't know who because I couldn't turn around to see.

As we trekked diligently down, I sensed something odd happening. The walls of the tunnel began to narrow, closing in on me with each step. My shoulders, too broad for the passage, began twisting sideways. Soon, I was walking crablike, lurching from side to side, which in my rotated posture had become back to front. They should have a sign outside the entrance, like at an amusement park:

If your shoulders are this wide, you can't enter.

Either that, or:

Abandon Hope, All Ye Who Enter Here.

I lurched down and down and down. Soon the ceiling of the tunnel seemed to be shrinking as well. Visions of Alice down the rabbit hole filtered into my uneasy imagination (Drink This). Little by little as I descended into the pit, my neck began to tilt sideways, forced lower and lower, until eventually my ear almost rested on my left shoulder. Ducking my head while twisting my shoulders, soon I was moving down the tunnel like the humpbacked assistant in a Frankenstein movie. Or loping like a crooked ape man with arms dangling askew, a Paleolithic Groucho Marx.

This sight could not have been comforting to the people walking behind me (unless they were walking the same way). As for those in front of me, everyone seemed to have a stride appropriate to their place on the evolutionary scale. The little girl seemed completely unaware of any problem except boredom.

I was not bored.

I was petrified.

The tunnel seemed to go on endlessly, mile after mile under the dark ponderous earth. Though terrified of heights, I've always been relatively comfortable in depths. So an attack of claustrophobia, a.k.a. the inescapable apprehension that there is a mountain suspended above your head, was completely unexpected.

The idea that part of us continues after death is older than history, probably because back then we lived in caves. There is nothing quite like a panic attack beneath a trillion tons of granite to pique your interest in immortality.

Down, always down, inexorably down, our guide marched us at an unrelenting pace. Only her steadiness kept me from running back up the tunnel (that and the people behind me). Sweat was beading on my forehead despite the coolness of the primordial depths. My heart was pounding, my breathing ragged.

After an hour (or possibly three minutes) of descent into oblivion, the stone passage widened into the cave proper. My panic did not completely subside, but at least I could stand upright and breathe normally again.

No one else on the tour exhibited any fear of anything, except possibly me. Once in the cave proper, the others gave me a wide berth, I hope because they sensed my discomfort and not because they thought they were trapped under a mountain with a heavy-breathing sideways-loping maniac.

I was willing to pay much more to leave the cave than I had paid to enter. But that wasn't necessary, for soon the tour was over and we returned topside. Once more in the safety of the gift shop, I bought another Coke (12 oz.) to settle my stomach.

My immediate memories of Rushmore cave were somewhat blurry, most likely because I had been concentrating my keen mental superpowers on reinforcing the limestone ceiling. So I purchased some souvenir postcards, to recall what I couldn't remember. From the postcards, I can tell it was a very nice cave, as caves go.

Having narrowly escaped the abyss of Rushmore the Cave, I looked forward to the broader vistas of Rushmore the Mount. The town of Keystone is situated at the base of Mount Rushmore.

I needed some time to recover both breath and poise after Rushmore Cave, so I decide to explore.

The small village turned out to be a tiny-but-worthy stop-and-shop site. The museum is dedicated to the creation of Rushmore and the years of labor, the delicate calculations, the successes and disappointments involved in carving the massive sculpture.

Mount Rushmore was named after a banker from the East who bought the mountain as an investment. He didn't realize apparently: mountains don't appreciate. After the gold ran out, local citizens hoped to attract tourists to the area, so they decided to carve a sculpture into the mountain (I can imagine that meeting–"Well, the gold is gone and we have all this dynamite. What do we do now?").

No one really took the concept seriously until 1927 when Calvin Coolidge visited the Black Hills. Coolidge, who shared many of the qualities of a statue, liked the idea and work soon began.

In the beginning, there was dissension over who or what should be depicted on the mountain. Finally they settled on four Presidents: Washington, Jefferson, Lincoln, and Teddy Roosevelt.

The memorial on Mount Rushmore was designed by a sculptor named Gutzon Borglum. Borglum studied in Paris, though I'm not sure how. As far as I know there are no mountains in Paris. Though maybe there are just none left. Eventually Borglum moved to South Dakota from Georgia, where he had been unhappy with his current mountain and the sheriff had been unhappy with him.

Borglum worked for years creating models of the sculpture. Finally, in 1934, the carving began. More than 400 people performed the dangerous and exacting labor of creating the sculpture. Ninety percent of the carving of the mountain was accomplished using dynamite. Over 450 tons of rock were blasted off, including a first draft of Thomas Jefferson, whose face was originally supposed to be on Washington's left (appropriate for a populist). The work was not completed until 1941, and Borglum died before he could see his masterwork finished.

The road to Mount Rushmore National Memorial wound up the mountainside, ending in a vast parking lot that that day was half-empty (or half-full). A multi-million-dollar renovation of the memorial had recently been completed, including a huge new stone entryway called the

Avenue of Flags, and of course the requisite visitors center and gift shop. Farther into the park, an amphitheater had been constructed, and, at the base of the sculpture, Borglum's studio had been renovated.

As I moved through the Avenue of Flags, my eyes went immediately to the faces on the mountain. From that vantage point, still some distance away from and below the sculpture, it was hard to get an idea of their magnitude. But the work was marvelously done, given the extraordinary scale. Certainly the memorial is an impressive engineering achievement.

Yet again, I had a feeling of disappointment. The faces, enormous as they were looked diminutive against the mountain. I had seen far more majestic and imaginative sculpture in the Badlands.

Even more disconcerting, the faces were all pointing in different directions. Roosevelt was staring at Lincoln, who was staring at Jefferson, who did not acknowledge Roosevelt in spite of the fact that Roosevelt and Jefferson appeared to be conjoined twins. Washington stared straight out, ignoring the lot of them. Viewed together, instead of statesmen united in a common vision of America's future, the four faces gave the disconcerting impression of men in a crowded public restroom trying desperately to avoid noticing one another.

I'm sure this was due to the exigencies of carving in granite and not a political comment. But the impression was political, or satirical, or both. As I gazed at Rushmore, images of the Macy's parade at Happy Hour kept floating into my head. Underdog would have fit right in.

Again maybe I expected too much, having lived near Washington DC. The Jefferson Memorial at night is exquisite and inspiring. Lincoln's lined impassive face in his memorial is austere and moving. The Wall of the Vietnam War Memorial is solemn and chilling.

But in the oddness, the distancing and unexpected feelings at Rushmore, I recognized something else. There were attempts at immortality evident at Rushmore: the immortality of the art; the immortality of the artist; the immortality of the legends; all set against the immortality of the stone, the mountain, the world, the universe itself.

Yet even the universe is doomed to a fiery implosion in the Big Crunch or a frozen expiration in the Big Whimper. And despite the Herculean efforts of man to achieve immortality, the artifact wouldn't last.

Sixty million years ago, a huge granite slab exploded out of the earth, creating the whole of the Black Hills. The stone is so hard that nothing but dynamite sufficed to carve the Rushmore memorial.

Yet scientists estimate that Rushmore erodes at a rate of one inch every 500 years. At that rate, Washington's face will be gone in (okay, 60 feet times twelve inches per foot equals 720 inches times 500 years equals) 360,000 years. That's a long time in human terms, far longer than the most generous estimates of the existence of our civilization. But it is only a blink in geologic time.

I had seen what wind and water could do in the Badlands, and what water alone could do in Rushmore cave. In fifty or a hundred million years, the Black Hills themselves may be gone, eroded by wind and water and tourists who spill Coke on the rocks. A hundred million years is a long time even geologically, but just a wink of the Universal Eye.

I turned away from the memorial and peered out from the mountain to where the curve of the world met the dome of the sky. Within that horizon, the circle of the sky in the circle of the eye, the cycle of transformation underlay everything.

Lichen and moss, flowers and trees, artists and tourists, all break down the rock. Over millions of years, soil is created. From the soil, vegetation emerges. From the vegetation, animal life proliferates. Then the waters come in and cover everything and the plants and animals die and get packed down into the bottom of the sea and over years and years harden into rocky layers. The layers are then lifted up into the air to make mountains and caves and everything starts again.

But in all that endless vital cycle, something would never change. I was there. I walked that path. I saw those faces. That was forever.

And I realized then. Time is a wave. The water is never the same from arc to trough. But everything the wave sweeps over changes it forever.

Everything that is will be lost.

Everything that's done is forever.

Maybe that's our soul, not what we are, but what we do.

*

*

A Transcendental Journey

*

In 1939, following his award-winning exhibit at the 1939 World's Fair, sculptor Korczak Ziolkowski (I promise I'm not making these names up) accepted a commission to carve a massive memorial on a mountain in the Black Hills to Lakota warrior and spiritual leader Crazy Horse. Ziolkowski worked briefly upstate at Mount Rushmore, then moved on to what became his life's work.

I knew little about Crazy Horse and less about the history of the region. But my father had always been fascinated by tales of the plains nations. So as I pulled in to the Crazy Horse site, I was looking forward to learning more.

The memorial site is managed by the Crazy Horse Foundation, which funds the carving exclusively through private donations and sales at the site. The master plan includes much more than the sculpture. Surrounding a courtyard, there's a visitors center (of course), a gift shop, a snack bar, an educational center and a museum.

Near the front of the courtyard, a stunning alabaster sculpture drew my attention: Crazy Horse rampant astride his horse, long hair trailing in the wind. His arm is outstretched with his finger pointing forward, seeming to lead his people into the future.

But the sculpture was merely a model for the gigantic one being carved into the mountain. Dominating the end of a granite ridge, the completed carving will be 563 feet high and 641 feet long, larger than all the presidents of Rushmore put together. The enormous undertaking will render the sculpture viewable for miles from three sides. This work would not be diminished by the mountain. It would be the mountain.

Next to the model was a legend that will also be carved into the mountain. The first sentence echoed Lincoln at Gettysburg:

> *Duty ours to place before the world a chronicle which will long endure.*

The text went on to explain that the Black Hills had belonged to *us* for *countless eons* before *murder, rape, and sanguine war* were suffered at the hands of the *invaders* and *greedy oppressors*. The inscription concluded with the grim heartrending words attributed to Crazy Horse: *My lands are where my dead lie buried.* I began to get the impression that the finger of Crazy Horse was not a guide but an accusation.

At the snack bar, I bought a normal-sized Coke, then strolled to the end of the courtyard to get a look at the mountain itself. Not much of the figure was identifiable then. The outlines of a body and horse were barely distinguishable, the face still rough and obscure. For a while, I watched the tiny figures of the workmen on the mountain. Then I wandered into the nearby Indian Museum of North America, also designed by Ziolkowski.

Sunlight flooded through skylights in the arched ceiling, making the lustrous bleached pine interior seem to glow. Native arts and crafts of exquisite workmanship and brilliant colors were exhibited throughout. It was an ethereal atmosphere in which to explore the history of a people.

High up on the museum walls, the words of Indian leaders surrounded us. Some were despairing, frustrated, resigned. But many evoked bitterness, rage, and hatred. The entire site was like an ancient curse enshrined in pine and granite.

The other tourists milled blissfully around the museum exhibits and browsed the marvelous crafts for sale, so maybe I was just still in a bad post-Badlands mood. But for me, the feeling was dissonance and, again, disappointment.

The beauty of the museum, full of light and color, contrasted severely with the pronouncements on the walls. The declarations disrupted, and finally dispelled, the tranquility and beauty of the building. Art in support of enmity is hard to support. Even beauty imbued with hatred is ugly.

Art can provoke, maybe has a responsibility to do so. Art can reveal suffering and expose injustice. But when the message overpowers the aesthetic, art ceases. Without the aesthetic experience, there is no art (sorry, conceptual non-artists). And that experience depends on the lowering of barriers, on joining, not dividing.

There are few enough mechanisms in this world that connect. They should be used with care. At Crazy Horse, art and beauty, subsumed in polemic, were rendered discordant. I left quickly, anxious to get away.

Yet the glorification of men of war continued as the theme of the day. I headed south, threading my way through Custer State Park.

It was certainly an odd juxtaposition, Custer and Crazy Horse. Then again, the titans of Rushmore were all famous in part for their roles in the general slaughters of the times. Everywhere I looked, the human contribution to the extraordinary landscape seemed negative. I began to feel ashamed for my species.

Even the ironic serenity of Custer State Park, and the discovery of another small herd of buffalo, this time ranging free, didn't lighten my mood. Maybe this was why the hills were called black.

Hot Springs is a small town at the southern end of the Black Hills. In years past, a well-known spa (the Evans Hotel to be exact) had made the geothermal pools famous, and there were still many little hotels where you could enjoy the healing benefits of a mineral bath.

In my darkened mood, I could have used some healing. But I really wanted to see the mammoths.

The Mammoth Site is a unique paleontological excavation in Hot Springs. Digging at the site is confined to the month of July, but you can visit year round.

The entire site was enclosed by a beautiful wooden building with a vaulted roof, strangely similar to the museum at Crazy Horse. But there was no anger or bitterness there, only a distant serenity, appropriate for what was essentially a mausoleum.

After ten minutes, the tour started. Our guide was a graduate student in paleontology with a sprightly manner and an ironic sensibility. She directed our group around the elevated walkway that surrounded the site so we could view the remains from all perspectives.

Over fifty mammoth skeletons have been uncovered at the site, along with wolves, llamas, bears, and other Ice Age animals. Some of the finds remain in-situ, only partially exposed. As we strolled around the dig, our guide explained the events that had trapped so many poor animals.

Twenty-five thousand years ago, mammoths and other Ice Age mammals roamed the slopes and meadows of the Black Hills. One day, at the southern end of the hills, a cavern collapsed (see, I knew it). A sinkhole formed, 150 feet wide and 60 feet deep, and filled slowly with water from an artesian spring at the bottom.

For the next 700 years or so, mammoths were lured into the sinkhole by the water collecting in the bottom. Once in, the huge beasts were unable to escape up the slippery sides. Trapped, they either drowned or starved to death and their remains collected in the base of the pit.

Over the years, silt filled up the sinkhole and the site was preserved under layers of mud. Twenty-five thousand years is not enough time for bones to fossilize completely, so the mammoth remains were preserved nearly intact.

As our charming guide delighted in telling us, all of the mammoths found at the site were male. Most likely they had been driven out of the pack, unable to breed, doomed to starve and die alone.

I don't even need to say it, do I?

I left the Mammoth Pit and drove back to Rapid City. Since it was already 6:00 PM, I checked back into the same motel, hoping my favorite desk attendant would again be attending. No such luck.

So I sat in my room, ordered some pizza, and opened my copy of Emerson. I read some of *Spiritual Laws*, a bit of *History*, then settled in to read *Experience*. Once again Emerson begins the essay with a few lines of poetry, this time with a slightly more ominous edge. He follows this with a haunting image:

> *"We wake and find ourselves on a stair; there are stairs below us, which we seem to have ascended; there are stairs above us, many a one, which go upward and out of sight."*

I knew then I was not in for the bravura of *Self-Reliance* nor the contemplation of *The Poet*. Something darker, and strangely fitting my strange mood, was at hand.

Emerson was the apostle of enthusiasm; nothing great is ever accomplished without it, he famously proclaimed. Emerson's optimistic outlook on life and his certainty that truth was immanent in nature are enshrined in his essays. His epigrammatic style reflected the unshakeable belief that life was both comprehensible and joyful. His pronouncements seem audacious in this skeptical age.

Yet the life of Ralph Waldo Emerson is a chronology of sorrow and loss. When he was eight years old, Emerson lost his father. After only two years of marriage, Emerson's beautiful twenty-year-old wife Ellen died of tuberculosis. His brothers Charles and Edward died soon after from the same disease. Henry Thoreau died of it at age 45. Emerson's brother Bulkeley was institutionalized much of his life. Margaret Fuller, Emerson's intellectual match, drowned with her husband and young child, shipwrecked on a sandbar within sight of land. And most devastating of all, Emerson's son Waldo died of scarlet fever at age five.

This is the paradox of Ralph Waldo Emerson: the joy of his vision versus the sorrow of his life. In *Experience*, Emerson denies his grief with grim intellect:

> *"Grief too will make us idealists. In the death of my son, now more than two years ago, I seem to have lost a beautiful estate,—no more. I cannot get it nearer to me. If to-morrow I should be informed of the bankruptcy of my principal debtors, the loss of my property would be a great inconvenience to me, perhaps, for many years; but it would leave me as it found me,—neither better nor worse. So is it with this calamity: it does not touch me; something which I fancied was a part of me, which could not be torn away without tearing me nor enlarged without enriching me, falls off from me and leaves no scar. It was caducous. I grieve that grief can teach me nothing, nor carry me one step into real nature. The Indian who was laid under a curse that the wind should not blow on him, nor water flow to him, nor fire burn him, is a type of us all. The dearest events are summer-rain, and we the Para coats that shed every drop. Nothing is left us now but death. We look to that with a grim satisfaction, saying There at least is reality that will not dodge us."*

Yet in *Threnody*, his elegy on the death of his son, an anguished Emerson contradicts himself:

"O child of Paradise!
Boy who made dear his father's home
In whose deep eyes
Men read the welfare of the times to come;
I am too much bereft;
The world dishonored thou hast left;
O truths and natures costly lie;
O trusted, broken prophecy!
O richest fortune sourly crossed;
Born for the future, to the future lost!"

After the death of his wife Ellen, Emerson walked to her tomb nearly every day. One day, more than a year after her death, he entered the tomb and opened her coffin. His journal entry for the day says nothing about what he saw or felt there. But I sometimes imagine that what he brought away from Ellen's tomb was expressed at the end of *Threnody*, when an answer to Emerson's cry issues from the "*Deep Heart*":

"Silent rushes the swift Lord
Through ruined systems still restored,
Broad-sowing, bleak and void to bless,
Plants with worlds the wilderness,
Waters with tears of ancient sorrow

Apples of Eden ripe to-morrow;
House and tenant go to ground,
Lost in God, in Godhead found."

Perhaps somewhere there was a mountain from which life could be seen that way. I had not found it in the Black Hills.

*
*
*

For a male of any primate species, all problems are solved by changing location. If the food runs out, move. If there are not enough females, move. If, Move is encoded in our DNA. However, the essential flaw in the Travel solution is this: No getaway gets you away from you.

I realized that somehow my excursion had gradually shifted. I wasn't the happy traveler I had envisioned, sightseeing by day and writing by night. I was having thoughts. Worse, I was having feelings. Worse than worse, I was not writing anything, except an occasional email.

I needed a vacation from my vacation.

So in the morning, I combed my brochures to find somewhere completely fun and mindless to counteract all of the annoying thinking and feeling. When I opened the brochure for Deadwood, I knew my problem was solved.

Deadwood had casinos. Casinos had gambling. I loved gambling. Actually, I loved winning, but in my imagination they were the same. So in the morning, I drove the fifty miles or so northwest to Deadwood.

It was a beautiful Saturday and apparently everyone else in South Dakota was also looking for mindless entertainment. I parked in one of the last spaces at the bottom of Main Street and began working my way up looking for a place to stay. Occasionally, I accidentally dropped a few coins in a slot machine.

I finally found a room at a casino at the top of Main Street, not far from the Silverado Casino, which was owned by Kevin Costner. I thought about staying at the Silverado, but I felt unsure of my welcome after the whole Cisco fiasco.

Deadwood was well named. The town lies in the northern end of the Black Hills, in a canyon cut by Whitewood creek. Settlers found the gulch filled with blackened and dying trees. Who would build a town in a valley of dead trees? On the other hand, maybe that's the perfect place to build.

In the 1870s, Deadwood boasted a dandy assortment of saloons, brothels, and Chinese laundries. At the time, two of Deadwood's most prominent citizens were James Butler Hickok and Martha Jane Canary, better known as Wild Bill and Calamity Jane.

Calamity Jane worked as a scout for the army, a Pony Express rider, and a stage coach driver among other occupations. Rumors linked her romantically with Wild Bill Hickok.

Hickok came to Deadwood in 1876, hoping to earn enough money to support his new bride, who was not Calamity Jane. While playing poker in Saloon #10, he was shot in the back (again not by Calamity Jane). At the time, Hickok was reportedly holding two pair, Aces and Eights, which has since become known as the Dead Man's Hand. Deadwood's citizens were better than average at names, at least as far as death was concerned.

After the gold rush faded, Deadwood became a sleepy and not too profitable town until the 1990s, when gambling was again legalized in South Dakota. Now the town is filled from top to bottom with casinos. I didn't see any Chinese laundries, or brothels, not that I was looking.

The casino where I was staying did not offer either dice games or poker. But they did have 100 or so slot machines spread over three smoky rooms, which was fine with me (the machines, not the smoke).

Most slot machines today are video slots, complex computers that simulate the rolling wheels of the old style mechanical slot machines, the kind we had when I was growing up in Maryland. I can remember the thrill of playing the nickel machines, waiting for the Bump, Bump, Bump of the wheels. The last wheel always bumped loudest. Three plums won you twenty nickels, which seemed like a fortune then.

Video slots have computer chips inside. These chips generate random numbers to determine where the simulated wheels will stop. In addition to these random numbers, a virtual weight (the kind I wish I had) is assigned to each position on the simulated wheel. This allows the casino management to control the probabilities and hence the amount paid out over time.

The Oracle of Delphi and Nostradamus are playing poker. Before the game starts, the Oracle pays Nostradamus what he's going to win. At dawn, they leave without speaking, already knowing when the next game will be held.

Different states have different regulations controlling how much the machines must pay out. The amount is usually expressed as a percent. For example, a machine may pay out 97.5% of the money inserted. Payouts are often advertised to draw customers to high-paying slots. If the percentage is less than 100%, you will lose eventually. Probably.

I once hypothesized that I could control the random number generator in the slot machine by concentrating my mental superpowers through Bernard's antlers. But in Deadwood, Bernard stayed in the room, so we will never know. Probably.

Random number generation is a complex science, useful in both slot machines and cryptology (the science of not knowing). Random numbers can be generated in one of two ways. A software program can use an algorithm (a series of instructions to the computer) to generate a seemingly random number. This is known as Pseudo-Random Number Generation, or PRNG. Alternately, a hardware generator can be used to sample some natural process. The generated noise is converted to a random series of integers. This is known As Hardware Random Number Generation, or HRNG. Coincidentally, PRNG and

HRNG are the exact noises made by the old mechanical slots.

Freud and Jung are playing five-card stud. Jung gets four Jokers and folds because he refuses to associate with that archetype. Freud nods off and dreams about sleeping with the Queen.

I spent much of the night playing the quarter slots and trying to catch the waitress' attention (they serve VERY small cokes in casinos). For hours in the smoky Deadwood hall. I watched the pseudo-wheels spin in pseudo-randomness, trying to predict the random appearances of the pseudo-waitress.

And I began thinking about how my random numbers were almost invariably losers. The whole process was beginning to seem not so random.

Randomness is unlikely. It's also a sloppy way to run a universe. For an event to be random, there must be no way to predict an individual outcome. But that is not the same as saying that, if there is no way to predict the outcome, the event must be random. This logical transition is known as the Fallacy of the Double No-No, or something like that. The contrary of the something doesn't imply the contrary of the other thing. (It's been a long time since I studied logic, which I'm sure you have already deduced.)

An alternate theory is that:

1) There is a controlling process.
2) Just because we can't observe the process doesn't mean it doesn't exist.
3) Never play poker with a mathematician.

Einstein, Podolsky, and Gödel are playing Deuces Wild. Podolsky gets three Aces, which he claims are the statistically predictable results of the unknown properties of playing cards. Gödel objects that the number three is not valid, since arithmetic cannot be represented by a complete and consistent logical system. Einstein rings a Bell and goes back in time. He deals himself four deuces and wins.

The characters of Einstein, Podolsky, and Gödel were featured in a movie called *IQ* (though they played badminton instead of poker). In the movie, an auto mechanic pretends he is a genius in order to win with the heart of mathematician Meg Ryan. Like that helps. I couldn't even get the casino waitress to talk to me.

Then a high-pitched voice queried:

"Another Coke?"

STEPHEN EVANS

There's just no telling with voices.

Chapter Four

Nature

The next morning, after a leisurely breakfast served by my now favorite waitress (who apparently did not require much sleep either), I was in an excellent mood. Deadwood had been the perfect antidote for my declining spirits.

I started the day wandering around northwest South Dakota searching for the geographical center of the country. The center (of the fifty states, not the contiguous forty-eight) was supposed to be 17 miles west of Castle Rock, which was supposed to be maybe 50 miles north of Deadwood. But I was again in a searching quandary.

What does the center look like?

Like everyplace else, only more so?

How do you find the center of something too big to see?

Drawing on my newfound wisdom in the ways of the quest, I kept my parameters flexible. Yet as so many politicians have discovered, the center of the country was elusive. There's never a monument around when you need one.

Eventually I wandered into Wyoming on Route 24, roughly following the course of the Belle Fourche River through Black Hills National Forest. Soon the flat farm country of northern South Dakota began to undulate, reforming into hills, until finally the road curved around and opened up onto miles of open plain. And there it was, fixed in uncanny solitude on a broad rise curving over the surrounding country.

I first learned of Devil's Tower in 1977 in the movie *Close Encounters of the Third Kind* when Richard Dreyfuss sculpted the image out of mashed potatoes. In the movie, the tower was a rendezvous point, a landing pad for alien visitors who were returning some borrowed people.

At the time, I was dating a girl who liked to smoke marijuana. We sat acutely stoned in the first row of the cavernous Uptown Theater in Washington DC, peering almost directly up at the screen. During the entire movie, we hunkered in our seats, terrified and giggling and devouring popcorn like crazy. I never smoked again.

In 1906, Theodore Roosevelt designated Devil's Tower as our first National Monument. Even I couldn't miss this one.

From my vantage point, still miles away from the Tower, it was impossible to tell exactly how big it was. But it was big and it was eerie: a huge craggy cone with deep creases running up and down its surface.

I pulled over to the side of the road to clean my glasses. I hate watching a smudgy world. The slightest mote of dust on my lenses sends me into paroxysms of cleanliness (though my obsession does not extend to other areas of housekeeping.)

By the second grade, I was already nearsighted from years of reading late into the night, holding the books inches away from my little orange nightlight. (Parents, let your kids stay up as late as they like as long as they are reading.) My first pair of glasses had bulky black frames and thick glass lenses—not exactly coke bottles but close enough. I was bigger and stronger than most kids my age, so I was spared the taunts of four-eyes and the like. But four eyes always sounded good to me, since I could read two books at once. It didn't work with two eyes. I had tried it.

I wear glasses all the time: to drive; to work; to read. A pane of glass consistently separates me from life (polycarbonate now, but you get the idea). Over the course of a lifetime, this sequestration alters your personality.

For a writer, a lens is like a periscope into other people's lives, allowing you to observe covertly while being emotionally concealed behind a glassy glare or tint. There is a classic scene in the movies where one lover removes the other's glasses. For those who wear glasses, this act is both tender and exquisitely erotic.

Without glasses, everything flows. Lines soften, distinctions mellow, colors thrill. And every light is a spotlight pointed at you, albeit a fuzzy one. The deglassified lover is transformed, intimately vulnerable and ultimately revealed. If both lovers are wearing glasses, the scene should not be viewed by children under 17.

Hiding behind a lens helps in other ways too. Sitting, observing, thinking, expressing: these are a writer's process, or mine at least. But you must be outside looking in, which might explain why I hadn't written a word on the journey: I kept driving into life.

Glasses can also be a liability, especially for a performer. On stage, lenses catch the glare of the lights, shielding the actor's eyes. That's why stage glasses have no lenses. I've tried wearing contacts. But after a few hours, my eyes mutiny, growing red and swollen from dryness or allergies or the fear of no longer being separate.

I've considered the laser surgery that reshapes your cornea. But I'm afraid of it. In part, I'm afraid of losing my eyesight. But I think I'm also afraid of losing that comfortable separation. It's odd to be afraid of what you long for.

Without my glasses, I squinted at the gnarled eastern face of Devil's Tower. Bizarre images flashed to mind.

The burial mound of a Titan.

A Brobdingnagian Caesar imprisoned in the earth, only his enormous pate visible above the surface, flat-topped and laurel-crowned and creased with the cares of empire.

A child's sandcastle a thousand feet high with serrated sides from an enormous scalloped bucket.

A gigantic subterranean dolphin with a tree-capped dorsal fin.

Or an alien landing area.

If I were an alien, I would head for Devil's Tower. No matter how fantastic my appearance, I'd be sure to blend in.

Replacing my glasses, I followed the road north. The road leading to the Tower was as aimless as the Belle Fourche River that it crossed, as if it kept changing its mind about approaching the monolith.

I passed a nearly deserted campground (wondering again if I should have brought camping equipment). Next door, at a combination general store/post office/snack bar, I stopped and bought a Coke (16 oz.) and some souvenirs. The road then carried me east over the river, before turning south, where I again pulled over by the side of the road.

To the left, away from the Tower, a prairie dog metropolis covered acres of the flat terrain. Residents without number scuttled and scurried as busily as their chubby bodies allowed, finishing their daily chores before gathering en mass to worship at the monolith or commune with the aliens.

Here I realized was a remnant of the vast prairie dog empires that had dominion over the prairie for thousands of years before man arrived (on their voyage up the Missouri River in 1804, Lewis and Clark reported seeing one that covered an entire valley). I hoped that I was seeing the re-emergence of this enlightening species.

Unlike the community in the Black Hills, signs posted every twenty feet or so warned not feed the animals. Apparently, human food is hard for them to digest. Maybe that's why Lloyd rejected my peanuts—he knew better.

Past the prairie dog town, the road changed its mind again, curving north along the western face of the Tower. At the point where the road finally began to ascend, a solitary deer grazed calmly in the median strip. I expected her to bound away as my car approached, as any Eastern relation surely would have. But she never flinched as I passed only a few feet away from her.

The road ended finally at the omnipresent visitors center. As usual, the facility was spotless, the employees friendly, and the exhibits informative. The National Park Service doesn't get enough credit for a difficult job well done. Imagine trying to manage all those millions of square miles of parks (not to mention keeping track of all the monuments).

Devil's Tower is an anomaly. No one is absolutely sure what it is or how it got there. The Tower is not smooth. On every side, enormous hexagonal columns of rock line the face from top to bottom. These rough-hewn pillars climb vertically more than 800 feet into the air, forming massive striations (the bear claw marks) in the Tower's appearance.

Sometimes, columns topple in thunderous avalanches, victims of time and erosion. At the foot of the Tower, mounds of boulders testify to cataclysms past.

One guess as to its origin is that the monolith is what remains of a long extinct volcano (though there is no evidence of lava flows or volcanic ash in the area). Another theory is that the Tower is a column of igneous rock that extruded through the sedimentary layers surrounding it. Over millions of years, the softer sedimentary rock around it eroded, exposing the tougher core.

The Plains Indians tell different tales of the monolith's rise. In one legend, seven girls were playing near the lair of a monstrous bear, who chased the girls onto a rock. Seeing the girls in peril, the Great Spirit raised up the rock to save them. As the stony surface rose into the sky, the bear clawed the sides, creating the deep indentations. Finally the girls were transformed into stars, set in the heavens as the Pleiades, the Seven Sisters constellation.

A path encircles the Tower (of course), one of several trails leading throughout the thirteen-hundred acre park. Ready to stretch my legs, I packed Bernard and my camera in my knapsack and headed toward the base.

Signs again warned me to stay on the path, as many Indian nations consider Devil's Tower to be sacred ground. I saw evidence of this along the path: beautifully worked blankets laid as offerings. Religious rites are still performed at the Tower, including sweat lodge ceremonies and even the Sun Dance, a famous celebration that gave its name to a town not far away: Sundance, Wyoming, which gave its name to the Sundance Kid, who gave it to Robert Redford, who gave it to his ski lodge in Utah, which gave it to a film festival in Park City. Names get around.

Far up on the southern face of the Tower, I noticed two tiny colored sticks. Every once in a while, one of the sticks would move upward or sideways. With all their gear, they looked something like aliens. But I guessed that they were climbers, one maybe a hundred feet higher than the other. I couldn't tell whether the upper climber was a girl, but I was pretty sure the lower one wasn't a bear.

Climbers travel from all over the world to scale the several routes up the Tower. Bernard made the attempt (I have the photo), but we hadn't brought the proper equipment so he didn't get far.

With my fear of heights, I didn't consider trying to climb. Actually, I can't imagine wanting to. Climbing Devil's Tower is like scaling the Sistine chapel. It might be fun but you're missing the point.

The path around Devil's Tower is about a mile long and runs several hundred feet out from the base of the monolith. I began walking counterclockwise, following the trail through stands of Ponderosa pine. Once again, possibly because of the lateness in the season, I was alone on the path.

At the beginning, the thick clustering of trees eclipsed my view of the monument, so I strolled along enjoying the shade and the sylvan surroundings. Then I noticed the silence.

There was no noise.

Anywhere.

No cars revving. No people talking. Not even birds singing or squirrels chattering.

All noise had suddenly ceased, as though sound waves could no longer propagate through the air. Remember that scene in horror films, just before something bad happens, where they say:

"Listen."

"What?"

"It's quiet."

"Yeah."

"Too quiet."

Then all hell breaks loose?

It wasn't like that at all.

When I get stressed, which is often, I sometimes imagine myself in a peaceful surrounding, someplace where I feel safe and relaxed and at ease. Some are real. Some exist only in my imagination. The serenity of Devil's Tower that day exceeded any place I have known or imagined. Tranquility filled the air, palpable, powerful, and embracing, wrapping me like a child in a blanket.

A few hundred feet down the silent trail, the curtain of trees on my left opened up and I got my first close look at Devil's Tower. To see the top, I had to crane my neck as far back as it would stretch, which made the Tower look just like it did from the first row of the movie theater in 1977. From a distance, the name Devil's Tower may seem appropriate. But in the shadow of the monolith, disaster seemed unimaginable.

But as I continued on my solitary path, another sensation overtook the calm: I felt as though someone was watching me. The sensation wasn't scary, just odd. Sly. Mischievous. I was encircled by a bemused serenity, nudged from behind by an ironic vitality.

Many cultures have legends of a Trickster God: Hermes to the Greeks, Loki to the Norse, Eshu in Africa, Tenshu to the Japanese, Kokopelli to the Hopi (who like many tricksters played the flute).

The servant of the Trickster God is the Fool, another ancient archetype represented through history by the Wandering Fool of the Tarot, the Jester of Medieval courts and Shakespearean plays, the shamanic Heyoka, the Joker in a deck of cards, and even Chaplin's Little Tramp in silent film.

Comedy is a lens, an approach to the world, a tap on the shoulder that says things are not what you think. Comedy is a trick of names, joining subject with subject in laughter. A bridge between paths, comedy begins in fact but tends to truth.

As Dante knew, any journey to enlightenment is a comedy. Hamlet is a comedy with the wrong ending, as Stoppard rightly saw. One can't be tragic and self-aware. But Shakespeare was right too: Life is a comedy with the wrong ending. Hamlet laughs through his soliloquy. Buddha smiles.

I looked around me but saw no one. The feeling wasn't emanating from the monolith. It just was, all around me, jovial and intelligent, playful, perhaps roguish, possibly devilish, but above all joyful. Dryads playing hide and seek. Aliens amused in cosmic candid camera.

Sacred as I have said before is not a word I use readily. Pipestone, the Badlands, and the Black Hills were all called sacred. And certainly, each of those sites had an unusual character, and inspired a unique emotional response: Pipestone was mystical, the Badlands majestic, the Black Hills profound.

Maybe it was my self-imposed anthropomorphism on a massive scale. Or maybe I was sensing a reflection of myself. Bemused serenity fits my public persona at least, and I've been described as Buddha-like (because of my mysterious smile I'm sure). But Devil's Tower felt alive.

There are two paths around the world, like the paths around the lakes in Minneapolis. One surrounds the other. Both surround what is real. Each path carries us in a different way.

These paths have been given many names throughout human history: for Emerson, Understanding and Reason; for Kant, Practical and Pure Reason; for Coleridge, Fancy and Imagination; for Heidegger, Ready-To-Hand and Present-To-Hand; for Merleau-Ponty, Sense and Nonsense. But they are all much the same. I think of them as Facts and Truth.

Facts are discrete, analytic, objective, functional, testable. Facts help us do things. Facts define Other.

Fact finding is a beneficial adaptation in our genetic construction. The capability developed with our minds eons ago, our genes creating the I for the eye. I and eye helped fulfill the function of reproducing our genetic material.

But genes build on what exists. Truth was our primordial relation to the world, our first path, which remains encoded deep in our genetic mechanism.

Truth is nonrational, synthetic, unifying, immersive. Truth isn't functional, because in truth there is nothing Else to function on. Truth is. Thou art that. Truth we recognize but can't pronounce. The recognition is the proof.

If this doesn't make sense, it's because it isn't sensible to use factual language to talk about truth. As Don Quixote says in *Man of La Mancha*, facts are the enemy of truth.

Sense and its recent progeny science so dominate our lives that we no longer acknowledge other cognitive paths. We have removed ourselves from the immediate world, cordoned ourselves in a Cartesian prison.

But we haven't warded ourselves thoroughly. Ladders at least hang over the prison wall: art and nature, poetry and comedy, can scale the fortress of our subjectivity, or perhaps tunnel under it, creating a path to apprehension. Maybe there are other paths as well, if we will look.

About a third of the way around the Tower, the pine trees on the outward side of the path were spaced well apart and you could see a good way into the forest. In a clearing a hundred yards away, a couple of animals foraged on the sunlit grass.

I didn't recognize them at first. They weren't devils, despite the prongs on their heads. They weren't aliens, having a distinct terrestrial appearance. They were quadrupeds, mammals of some sort. I finally guessed they were antelope.

The pair looked up at me for a moment and as with the deer I expected them to bound off into the forest. They didn't. They just kept looking at me.

Then I figured it out. This was the place. The site out of Western legend. Enshrined in the song. Where the buffalo roam. Where seldom was heard a discouraging word (or anything else for that matter).

Where the deer and the antelope play.

I wanted to play too. So much. But I didn't. I stayed on the path.

The antelope finally went back to grazing between the trees, gracefully wandering, like silent spirits at ease in their pine-scented stadium. I watched them, I don't know for how long, as they drifted farther and farther into the woods until I could barely make out motion against the scattered forest background. Then I forced myself to start walking again.

According to the Park Service, both mule deer and pronghorn antelope have been reported at Devil's Tower. No reports on who won the game.

It was afternoon and the northern side of the path was brighter and hotter than the eastern side, so I increased my pace. Soon, I made it all the way back around to the western side of the Tower and headed back to the parking lot. The walk had taken two hours, not the twenty minutes it should have. I felt like Jodie Foster in *Contact*, the hours of my journey unaccounted for.

Muddled and hot and smiling, I drove back to the park entrance and stopped at the snack bar, which looked like a redwood dairy queen. A menu was taped next to the little sliding glass window over the counter, listing the usual: hot dogs; snow cones; ice cream; espresso; cappuccino; latte...

I looked at that last again to make sure. It really said latte. Blame my Eastern prejudice, but a latte just wasn't what I expected at a snack bar in Wyoming. Lattes are my most serious addiction. I ordered a latte. I had to know.

My experiences at Devil's Tower were curiously serene: prairie dogs; mysterious monoliths;

quirky pines; the deer and the antelope. Yet the one that is most sensually forged in memory is the latte. Fresh. Steaming. Creamy. Frothy.

Try the Devil's Tower latte.

It's oddly perfect.

*
*
*

Somehow somewhere between Rushmore and Yellowstone, my little silver tape recorder began malfunctioning. Everything I taped during that period is completely unintelligible.

When I play those messages, the voice issuing from the recorder is impossibly deep and inhuman. It could be the sound of a Spirit from another Plane of Reality. It could be the voice of an Alien from another Galactic Cluster. Or it could be that I Accidentally Nudged the Speed Control. Anyway, if I Discovered the Answer to the Ultimate Question in Wyoming, we'll never know.

Rain glazed the Wyoming highway with a misty shimmer as I hydroplaned for an unknown time up and down the graceful swells of I-90. A diffused luster emanated from the saffron hills, illuminating the high drifting clouds, which echoed a brilliant yellow gray.

Through the windshield, the slick road cresting the billowing hills looked like a tongue beckoning me into the mouth of the world. In the rear view mirror, a band of tranquility coursed out across the plains from Devil's Tower.

After short stopping each day in the Black Hills, I was ready to cruise. Wyoming was the right state for that.

You could drive twenty minutes on the highway that day without seeing another car. In Washington DC, this would be considered evidence of divine intervention. And once again, most of my fellow wayfarers were faring the other way. Before it was unnerving. Now it was invigorating.

I passed through Gillette and Buffalo, winged through Crook and Campbell and Johnson counties, forded once more the meandering Belle Fourche, then the Powder and the Crazy Woman rivers, tracking the Bighorn Mountains all the way to Sheridan.

I stopped there for the night, a few miles from the Montana border, at a motel on a bluff overlooking the town. After dinner, I took

Waldo with me poolside. Mushroom hills cradled the lights of the city while mountains to the west held vigil over the sleepy town, as I read the essay *Nature*.

In 1836, Ralph Waldo Emerson published his first book, a little pamphlet entitled *Nature*. The short anonymously published volume established the foundation for the philosophical movement known as Transcendentalism.

Transcendentalism was an outgrowth of the German idealism of Immanuel Kant, a philosophy that developed in the late Seventeenth century as a response to the sensible thought of Scottish empiricist David Hume, who built on the work of the English skeptic John Locke, which was itself a response to the meditations of the French mathematician Rene Descartes. Philosophy at the time was an international sport, like soccer and politics today.

Immanuel Kant was the Clark Kent of Philosophy, a mild-mannered professor whose superpowered alter ego took the form of an arcane work called the *Critique of Pure Reason*. Kant's revolutionary intuition was that the mind actively organizes the information it gets from the senses, using categories such as time and space and causation to "make sense" of the raw sensory data.

Kant's radical principles shook the twin pillars of royalty and religion in Europe. His ideas and those of his Idealist successors came to England (and then to America and Emerson) through the writings of Coleridge, the Intellectual Romantic, and Carlyle, the Romantic Intellectual who would later become Emerson's proponent, antagonist, and devoted friend.

Emerson was a dedicated and eclectic reader. He absorbed the idealism of Kant and Schelling, the sacred texts of the Hindu, the ecstatic poetry of the Persians, the mysticism of Swedenborg, English Romanticism (Wordsworth, Coleridge), German literature (Goethe), and Roman and Greek philosophies (Plotinus and Plato). Combining all of these influences, Emerson somehow conceived a uniquely American philosophy called Transcendentalism.

Transcendentalism rests on two essentially American notions. First, the individual (not the institution) has the primary and inherent connection to the Universal. Second, nature is both the emblem and the apparatus of this spiritual connection.

With the possible exception of Nietzsche, Emerson is the most epigrammatic of modern philosophers. Yet transcendentalism had no commandments; the literature was the principle.

But if Thoreau's *Walden* can be considered the *New Testament* of Transcendentalism, the *Old Testament* is found in Emerson's little volume, *Nature*.

As is natural I suppose for a testament from Concord, the birthplace of the American revolution, *Nature* was a revolutionary manifesto. Rejecting answers and institutions from remote times and people and places, Emerson calls instead for a revelation both personal and immediate:

> *"Our age is retrospective. It builds the sepulchres of the fathers. It writes biographies, histories, and criticism. The foregoing generations beheld God and nature face to face; we, through their eyes. Why should not we also enjoy an original relation to the universe? Why should not we have a poetry and philosophy of insight and not of tradition, and a religion by revelation to us, and not the history of theirs?"*

In Dantesque ascension, and with a systemization found nowhere else in Emerson's work, the little volume analyzes the relationship between Spirit (God or the Over-Soul) and Nature (in Emerson's meaning, everything that isn't Spirit).

The essay entitled *Nature* that I read that night was not the 1836 pamphlet, but the distillation Emerson published in 1842 in his second series of essays. In the intervening years, Emerson had established his singular style of compressing the broadest truth into the fewest words with the greatest effect.

> *"That power which does not respect quantity, which makes the whole and the particle its equal channel, delegates its smile to the morning, and distils its essence into every drop of rain. Every moment instructs, and every object: for wisdom is infused into every form."*

It may seem odd, reading about nature during the overwhelming experience of it. But it was like having an intimate conversation with someone who had shared the same life-altering encounter, who knew what you were going through, who understood what it meant to you, who had undergone the transformation that was overtaking you. The essays at night transmuted the assays of the day. The reading made it real.

Each day on my journey a personal revelation unscrolled. And its wake, though I did not know it, slowly I was awakening. And imperceptibly, becoming.

The next morning, I got an uncharacteristically early start. I know it was early (for me) because the McDonalds outside Billings, Montana, was still serving breakfast.

At the time I was a lacto-ovo vegetarian, eating eggs and other dairy products. So for breakfast I had an egg biscuit and a SUPERSIZE coke. I'm an ethical vegetarian, not a healthy one.

Fog was rising off the surface of Lake of the Isles, so it must have been evening. There was no snow, so it must have been August. I was still in Minnesota, so I must have been married.

Hundreds of Canadian geese roamed the Minneapolis park around Lake of the Isles from early spring until they departed for more temperate climes in the late fall. I always enjoyed their company. But they did make something of a mess (literally) and I guess people complained.

A metal pen had been erected down by the shore, and several dozen geese were being held prisoner. One by one, workers were taking geese out of the pen and carrying them to a white panel truck with an unrecognizable but official-looking logo.

Most likely, they were being relocated to other areas around the state. Minnesota has many lakes, probably more than the proverbial ten thousand. The city of Minneapolis itself supposedly has 18 lakes, though I knew of only four. But as far as the geese knew, they were being kidnapped.

The workers were not gentle, but I imagine it's hard to be gentle when you have a full-grown goose struggling in your arms. As each bird was snatched away from the enclosure and hauled to the truck, it began to cry. Not squawk or honk or some other non-human word. Cry.

Our path to the world shapes us more than we know. The human world is a playground of objects, ready to hand for need or entertainment. To keep it that way, we shelter ourselves from the consequences and consciousness of our actions, insulated by institutions and traditions and worldviews that condone our marauding methodologies. Our indulgence is self-confirmed by need and greed.

My father was an artist with a carving knife. He grew up on a farm in Iowa and later worked as a cutter in meat-packing plants. I know he respected my compassion for animals, but I suspect it puzzled him too. Land and animals for him were something to live off, not something to live with. Except for dogs, of course, who were always accorded family membership.

Many people defend carnivorous behavior as part of their heritage. This argument has the rigor of a child's tantrum: Tommy did it, why can't I? The heritage argument is also selective. Our history also includes cannibalism and the Spanish Inquisition, but I don't hear much pining for them (unless you watch Monty Python or listen to Talk Radio). Killing animals for sport is cruel. Killing animals for food is (or should be) unnecessary. But it's more honest than a trip to the grocery store, or a McDonalds.

If morality is not convincing, you would think self-interest might be. We endanger ourselves each time we endanger animals. Throughout human history, when one group wants to control or destroy another, the first step is to name them: Animals, they say. Not really Human. Undeserving of rights, money, peace, freedom, life, or whatever else has become the object of acquisition.

The way we treat animals is the way we may one day be treated, even disallowing the possibility of reincarnation. In an enlightening episode of *The Twilight Zone* TV show, aliens invite humans to go to their home planet. An alien book falls into human hands and the title is translated as *How to Serve Man*. Too late, we discover it's a cookbook.

An alien invasion may be necessary to get us to change. It's a question of values, which is to say, a question without a rational answer. Ants have their values inbred in their antennae, which detect the morality of the nest by aroma. We humans conjure our values in survival mode out of our DNA, then decorate the consequences with nature's tools: logic, emotion, and five mere senses.

Moral argument is an oxymoron, a fallacy more pathetic than the Pathetic Fallacy. To be convinced, just watch the Sunday morning political talk shows. The technique is to start from a moral axiom and then erect a logical fortress around it. Since the starting points are not coherent, argument never ends in agreement, no matter what rational bridges we build.

In such an atmosphere, politics becomes the art of the possible and not the art of possibility. Already, this century (and the previous century and the one before that and the one before that) provides ample proof that humans can be convinced to commit any act, no matter how inconceivably horrible to others.

Nature teaches the tyranny of the gene, the tautology of the fittest. Nature cherishes process, the coming to be and the passing away. The Ten

Commandments were written on stone, not in stone.

To live is to choose. But we are a fortunate generation in this sense: new choices are available. We don't have to kill to survive. We don't have to despoil the land to acquire as much as we can against the winter's deprivations. This is the dawning of the Age of Aquarius.

The Anthropomorphic life is not easy. If I am ever arrested for drunk driving, it will be motoring down a country lane after sunset, swerving desperately to avoid the fireflies.

Each day, we choose: to kill or not to kill. Each day, I choose not to kill. The hopeful aspect is, this is something I have learned. I've never gone back and never regretted it. There are aspects of life we can't change. We need to pay attention to those we can. People can choose compassion, changing their lives, or at least the living.

It can be done.

*
*
*

The roads of Montana were a touch more crowded than Wyoming, and far less tranquil. At that time, the highways in Montana had no speed limit. I-90 was like an Autobahn for pickup trucks. My little four-cylinder Cavalier could cruise up to 85 miles per hour without too much rattle. I tried that for a while. It was fun but nerve-racking. Soon I settled back to the more comfortable 75 to 80 range. Most of the cars around me seemed to agree. Occasionally, someone would barrel by me at speeds I could only guess. But most were not in such a hurry.

The state of Montana is like two territories smashed into one another, each with terrain so different you can't believe they belong together. The eastern part of Montana is level like a Plains state. The western part is rugged and mountainous—definitely Marlboro country.

I-90 from Billings to Bozeman is a straight shot, following (though I didn't know it then) the path of the Yellowstone River. Towards the end of a long harrowing day of velocity, I made it to Livingston, Montana, a small city at the edge of mountain ranges. It was getting late but, spinning quickly through the quiet lanes of Livingston, I didn't see any place I wanted to stay.

Some friends had recommended a lodge called Chico Hot Springs about thirty miles to the south, so I headed there. If there was no room at the inn, I knew I'd be in trouble, because it would be late and I would have no other options. But I took a chance and headed for Paradise.

Paradise Valley is fifty miles of broad flat ranchland rising into the Absaroka Beartooth Range on one side and the Gallatin Range on the other. Billowing clouds clustered around the impassive peaks on either side like white-haired ladies playing bridge. Farms and ranches were planted sporadically down the heart of the valley.

Route 89 follows the Yellowstone River south through the Valley. Well, it doesn't follow it, it parallels it. The Yellowstone River flows backward, running north through the valley when any sensible river would be flowing south. In fact, the Yellowstone almost escapes to Canada, flowing northeast for hundreds of miles until it joins the Missouri in North Dakota. Watching the wrong-way course, I couldn't shake the odd feeling that the river was flowing up. Siddhartha discovered a retrograde river on his way to Nirvana. I had found one on the road to Paradise.

About twenty miles down the road, I turned off Route 89 and headed half a mile or so up the hillside to the resort at Chico Hot Springs. Built in 1906, the original building was beautifully maintained. The décor of the lobby had a rustic elegance I found welcome and surprising, not what I thought a lodge would be. The dining room, formally attired in white linen table cloths and burnished wood columns, promised more unexpected frontier elegance.

Several different kinds of accommodations were available in the old building, some European style with shared bathrooms and others on the American plan. The resort also had another building just a short walk away. Constructed relatively recently, the rooms had more comfort but less character. Chico Hot Springs is a popular getaway for Montanians. So even toward the end of September, I felt lucky that rooms were available. I selected a room in the new building and wasn't disappointed.

I am not ordinarily a poolish person. But my friends had also mentioned the unique swimming pool at Chico. Since I was still in the upper latitudes, there was plenty of light left after I checked in. So I put on my trunks and headed for water, winding my way through the labyrinth of corridors from the lobby to the pool. After a couple of wrong turns, I finally found my way.

At 5000 feet above sea level, it was a little high up and late in the year to be swimming outdoors at 8:00 at night. Fortunately, the source of the pool was an underground hot spring. The geothermally-heated water passed continually into and out of the pool, so neither heaters nor chemicals were needed.

The area contained two pools side by side. In the larger pool, the water temperature was a comfortable 96 degrees. In the smaller pool, a rectangle maybe 10 by 30 feet, the water was Jacuzzi-like at 104 degrees.

At that hour, few other guests were around. Most of them were kids, and I felt like one myself, restored to youth in a Rocky Mountain Shangri-La. Floating in the pool was easy, thanks to the mineral content of the water, not my body-mass index. I levitated in the large pool for twenty minutes, then bobbed in the smaller for a bit, then back, and so forth. French fries and a salad at the poolside snack bar comprised my dinner. Otherwise my regimen continued as long as the light lasted.

In my cabin, relaxed and peaceful, I fell asleep to the chuckling outside my window of the hot springs brook after a thousand-year journey to the surface trickling down to the contrary river, then on to the Missouri, the Mississippi, the

Gulf, and beyond. Everything flows everywhere I guess.

In the morning, the lodge laid out a huge buffet breakfast in the formal dining room, overflowing with scrambled eggs, a cornucopia of fruit served in a gargantuan crystal bowl, a variety of hot and cold cereals, and excellent coffee with sweet cream. It was lacto-ovo heaven.

After breakfast, I still had a few hours before checkout. Ignoring ingrained moral imperatives about swimming after meals, I went back to the pool. In the chill air of a Montana morning, I floated in the hot spring warmth, my arms spread wide, my head back and pointed skyward, my ears embraced in the moist hush of the gently percolating waters, my eyes closed and kindled by the cloudless sky. Immersed in hermetic oblivion, I prepared for the call of nature.

*
*
*

The next morning, I drove the thirty miles south to Gardiner. Just outside the Yellowstone gate, the tiny hamlet of Gardiner, Montana, is half quaint rural community, half rustic tourist attraction. The town was probably named for someone named Gardiner, though I never found out who he or she was. But as I drove down the main street of the town, I thought of the legendary Green Man: Neolithic Gardener, druid protector, Paul Bunyan with hoe instead of axe, Gabriel with spade instead of sword, an elemental steward tending the Empyrean Garden of Yellowstone.

Just a few hundred yards past Gardiner, a stone structure known as the Roosevelt Arch marks the northern entrance to Yellowstone National Park. As I drove beneath it, I felt like I was entering the land of Oz, except I was going under the rainbow, not over.

When you enter Yellowstone from the north, the first area you encounter is Mammoth Hot Springs. A century and more ago (not long after Yellowstone was designated our first National Park), an army encampment was established at Mammoth to protect the park from our more entrepreneurial (and less scrupulous) citizens. Now the soldiers are gone and the encampment has grown into a small village, with a lodge (one of four in the park), a ranger station and museum, and a restaurant, in addition to several park administration buildings. My knowledge of Yellowstone was limited to the twin images of geysers and grizzlies. So I stopped by the ranger station to take quick tour of the museum and collect some brochures.

Yellowstone covers 2.2 million acres of land, almost 3500 square miles, roughly the size of Rhode Island and Delaware combined. The park lies mostly in northwest Wyoming, but spills over into both Montana and Idaho. Yellowstone was our first national park, dedicated by President Ulysses S. Grant in 1872. Nearly three million people visit Yellowstone each year.

Bestriding the juncture of several fault lines, Yellowstone is the most active geothermal area in the world. Thousands of tiny earthquakes rattle the area each year, most imperceptible to humans. Major volcanic eruptions have occurred at Yellowstone in the past, a thousand times more powerful than the Mount St. Helens explosion.

These titanic Yellowstone eruptions emit pyroclastic flows, searing tsunamis of gas and rock surging at a hundred plus miles an hour with enough molten rock to cover the entire US. The last eruption created an enormous caldera (derived from the Spanish word for cauldron), a geologic feature that underlies much of the current park. Scientists have determined that these major eruptions occur roughly every 600,000 years and the next one is just about due.

Treading a touch more softly on the uncertain earth, I left the museum and immediately encountered two large animals grazing calmly on the lawn. They weren't deer or antelope this time; they were elk, the most common large mammal in Yellowstone and regular residents of Mammoth Hot Springs. The celebrity pair munched the lawn, unconcerned by the human paparazzi circling them.

If Mammoth Lodge was sitting on a volcano, you didn't notice it right off. So I decided to check in first and worry later. Inside the lodge, I inquired at the reservation desk. The clerk informed me that I was lucky to get any room without a reservation. At all. Ever. But it was my lucky day: several cabins just happened to be available.

Luck like everything else is relative. Built in the 1920s for that new breed, the motor tourist, the cabins reminded me of the ones I bypassed in the Badlands, perfect for the writing I wasn't doing. My cabin was small and spare, the bed little more than a cot. But I was content, being it was the wilderness and all. I unloaded my suitcase, and Bernard and I headed out for adventure.

Our first stop was the hot springs area, just a few hundred yards from the lodge. Like many areas of Yellowstone, the ground at Mammoth can crumble away beneath you without warning, plunging you into a scalding hot spring bath. Boardwalks have been built throughout the area to protect visitors; it's definitely not the place to wander off the trail, so I again kept to the path religiously, winding my way to the top of a ridge through a stand of fir trees. When I stepped out of the trees, I wasn't in Wyoming anymore. I was on Venus.

Limestone layers like alabaster terraces descended in succession down the rise, as if a cavern had surged out the earth and into the light of day. Within each layer, a shallow pool of vaporous fluid ebbed into the next pool below, step by delicate calcified step all the way down the ridge.

The hot springs at Mammoth are not simply pools of hot water. The volcanically heated water boils up from deep underground through limestone deposits, remnants of shallow seas that covered much of the western continent a hundred million years ago. The acidic water dissolves and collects limestone and minerals on the way up, then bubbles out through tiny openings in the top of the ridge.

As the water flows down the hill, it cools and deposits the limestone on the way. Algae in the pools tint the travertine, forming the remarkable spectacle visible today. Each pool displayed its own pastel palette over the gleaming white limestone.

I tried taking a few photographs, though I was sure that no picture of mine could capture the subtle tinctures and unworldly architecture. Often on my journey, I wished for a better camera, anything that might help me recall the splendor and wonder of these experiences. But a better camera might have been more distraction than enhancement. Eyes and memory are the best camera. I enjoy the photographs I took, but treasure the memories more.

Elk were not the only large mammals in the park, and the one Bernard and I most wanted to see was a moose. According to the pamphlets I unracked at the Ranger Station, the stretches of wetlands south of Mammoth were the closest areas for moose viewing. The best times were early mornings and late evenings. It was about midday, but we weren't likely to get up early anyway (well I wasn't, and I was driving). So Bernard and I left Mammoth and turned south, moosing in hope.

Yellowstone was supposedly named for the yellowish tint of the local rock. But contrary to rumor, the roads in the park are not made of yellow brick. The rumor may stem from the exceptionally bumpy passages. Frigid winters and hot crowded summers make the highways in Yellowstone difficult to maintain.

South of Mammoth, the road was closed, as a crew worked hard to get a few patches in before the first snow, which at that elevation (5,000 to 11,000 feet above sea level) could have arrived anytime. Even in September, a line of twenty or thirty cars had formed. Two thousand miles from the Washington beltway, I had still managed to find a traffic jam.

But something curious was happening. Instead of grumbling, cursing, and honking, most of the drivers (including me) got out of their cars and took advantage of the downtime to enjoy the spectacular roadside vista of valley, pond, forest, and mountains beyond. While up ahead the road crew poked and pitched and patched, we joked and waited and passed the time with the ranger who was stuck just like the rest of us. If I wasn't in Kansas, the congeniality of our little corps of explorers proved I wasn't in DC anymore either.

After an amiable quarter hour, we got back in our cars and slipped by the smiling construction crew. Beneath his hard hat, the gangly worker directing traffic might have had hair the color of straw.

A few minutes down the road, Bernard and I spotted a sign:

Willow Park
Watch for Moose

The clearing, on a small rise, commanded a broad view of a wetland area spread out to the west, opening up onto a large lake maybe a mile away. An unguessable distance beyond were the peaks of western Yellowstone, snow-capped mountains barely visible in the haze.

Binoculars in hand, we surveyed the wetlands for signs of moose. Sadly they never showed. A large bird soared over the lake, then turned west to the mountains beyond. By the time I got out my camera, the bird was just a dot in my viewfinder and I couldn't tell what species it was. Eagles, osprey, and hawks can all be seen in Yellowstone. If it was a hawk, it was an especially large one to be visible at that distance.

Bernard and I quested for moose in several more spots along the road that day. They remained elusive, unwilling to greet their cousin from the East. But the chipmunks entertained us while we waited, so it wasn't a complete loss.

Yellowstone has its own grand loops of highway, a figure eight that crisscrosses through the developed area of the park. Disappointed by moose, we continued south down the northwest loop, then cut eastward across the middle of the figure eight. Our next destination was the Grand Canyon of the Yellowstone, and the famous waterfalls.

On both sides of the road, forest fires had ravaged the park. In 1988, uncontrolled fires incinerated almost 800,000 acres, more than a third of the forests of Yellowstone. Blackened ground and burned out husks of trees still dominated vast areas of the park.

Fire is considered an important tool in park management (by park management, not the animals and plants, I imagine). Since 1988, the role of fire in the life cycle of the wilderness had been debated (I won't say hotly). Experts tell us that forest fires return minerals to the soil and create new lairs and food sources for birds and animals. Pinecones burst in the intense heat, spreading seeds across the forest floor. This cycle was visible even from the road. In the shelter of torched remnants, saplings beyond count had emerged, thrusting through the charcoal earth. Most were only a few inches high. But the forest was healing itself.

Down the road, a number of cars had pulled onto the shoulder by a broad meadow. Assuming there was something worth seeing (always a good assumption in Yellowstone), I joined the small crowd lined up along the gravel roadside. A hundred yards away, oblivious to the attention he was drawing, a wolf pup was playing in the meadow.

Even in Yellowstone, encountering a wolf was amazing luck. Years of hunting and human encroachment had at one time all but eliminated wolves from the continental US. But in 1995, despite protests from local ranchers, a Park Service program had reintroduced several families of wolves into Yellowstone.

This little guy was maybe a third of the size of a full-grown wolf, and was as cute as any mammal at that age. He was all alone as far as we could see, and seriously playing. He would crouch down low to the ground, almost hidden in the tall grasses, sneak forward a few feet, then leap suddenly at his imaginary prey. He performed this ritual over and over.

I watched for half an hour at least, then finally, dragged myself away and hurried on toward the Grand Canyon of the Yellowstone. The canyon is the most famous vista in the park, the subject of a well-known painting by Thomas Moran that hangs in the Capitol building in Washington DC. Moran's watercolor sketches, produced during an 1871 expedition to the area, helped convince Congress to make Yellowstone our first national park.

There are several places to view the canyon, but I choose Inspiration Point, a famous spot where a rocky promontory projects out beyond the normal line of the canyon wall, making it easy to see for miles both upstream and downstream. From the swarming parking lot, I followed the crowd out onto the promontory. Then I stopped breathing.

Yards away, the sheer canyon wall plunged down a thousand feet or more. My mind projected the event over and over in slow motion: sliding to the ground, rolling to the edge, tumbling over the precipice, bouncing off the trees, and splatting on the boulders far below.

I am a descendant of the kings of Scotland (and I'd like it back, thank you), so you would think I might have inherited a Highland gene or two. But apparently not. My mother was also afraid of heights. And she hated seafood and loved potato chips, as I do. As we learn about our genomic architecture, I suspect more and more of human behavior will be attributed to DNA. It is not in our stars, but in our cells, that we are queasy.

I was frozen in terror. But as usual, the people around me felt nothing of my fear. While I stood quaking on the rocky cliff, everyone else strolled blithely out to the rim and leaned over the railing to enjoy an unobstructed view of the grandeur of the canyon and the falls beyond. Some perched far out on the rocks, just a teeter (or totter) away from doom.

I closed my eyes and steadied myself. I had driven three thousand miles to see this sight. Nothing was going to make me miss it. But my knees did not agree.

But my feet are braver than my knees. Slowly they inched toward the brink of the precipice. Each time someone brushed past me, I winced and halted, desperately wanting to sink down right where I was, close my eyes, and crawl back to my car. My feet lurched forward, never leaving the ground, hugging the rocky surface. At any moment, I imagined, the ledge would give way and I would plunge to my death. But bracing myself on the metal railing, shuffle by stiff halting terrified and excruciatingly cautious shuffle, I managed to move onto the upper level of the viewing platform.

Out on the platform, my fear was subsumed by the astonishing spectacle. I still felt terrified. I just didn't care as much. It was the aesthetic experience on the grandest scale. There was nothing to do but see, and the seer was the least of the equation.

Over thousands of years, natural forces (including the Yellowstone River, which flows through and out of the canyon), have carved an enormous v-shaped chasm deep into the mountains. At the south end of the canyon, the current drops hundreds of feet into the canyon basin in two magnificent torrents. The Upper Falls descend straight down over one hundred feet. The Lower Falls plunge more than three hundred feet to the canyon floor. To the north, the still backward river flows, shining for miles past the sharp-edged mountains, winding through the base of the cleft on the way to Paradise.

After a few moments absorbed in the splendor of the canyon, I recollected myself and, becoming fearful (or sensible) again, shuffled quickly back to my car. Breathing normally (for me) once more, I drove out and north, heading around the northeast loop to get back to Mammoth and the security of my cabin.

But my Yellowstone travails weren't over. The highway in Yellowstone was appropriately named: high way. Mammoth was already 6000 feet above sea level, and from there the road runs along slopes from a hundred to several thousand feet higher. The western side of Yellowstone was fairly mild driving. The eastern side was a severe test for the acrophobic.

The bumpy road kept climbing and climbing, winding higher up into the mountains. Hint for driving mountain roads: closing your eyes doesn't help.

Finally I pulled around a curve and discovered a snack bar under siege by a horde of cars. No abyss was in sight and the day had grown hot, so I stopped and bought an ice cream bar. Behind the snack bar, a path led down and around a hill, so I trekked down, once more following the crowd. Melting ice cream in one hand, napkins in the other, I was fully prepared for whatever dairy emergency I might encounter.

In a clearing the bottom, I found another waterfall, one of nearly 300 or so cascades in the park. A tiny stream toppled over a rocky cliff into a small pool about forty feet below. Up and down the face of the cliff, people were perched on the rocks, enjoying the spray as the plunging brook splashed over the crags.

Unfortunately, all the good crags were taken and that was enough of crowds for me. I quickly slurped the rest of my ice cream, walked back to the car, and drove down the road a ways. Fortunately, it was down this time. At no particular point, and for no particular reason, I pulled over, got out of the car, and began walking downhill through a thicket of trees. At the bottom, I found a massive meadow many football fields wide, extending lengthwise in either direction farther than I could see. According to my ranger map (compass decoder ring sold separately), the meadow stretched for miles, all the way back to the village at Mammoth Hot Springs.

I was alone. There were no tourists, no boardwalks, no trash cans, no sign of human existence at all. Amid the tall grasses, wildflowers glowed like tourmaline in the amber afternoon sun. Now and then a solitary sapling offered some shade to the insects buzzing around.

I thought of my Badlands flower, alone and unnoticed under the juniper trees. How much worse to be this botanic miracle with no one but the occasional antisocial escapee to appreciate such bounty? And how many other such meadows were there in a park the size of a state or two?

I sat in the shade on the hillside and enjoyed the meadow, and imagined that the meadow enjoyed me. When the sun started sinking, I drove back to my cabin to get ready for dinner.

After a shower, my hair dryer seemed to be making a curious sound, a weird keening noise over and above the usual whine. I turned it off. The moaning grew louder, but now I could tell it was coming from behind my cabin: a hollow, eerie wailing echoing like an army of flying monkeys, and large full-throated monkeys with vocal training at that.

I ran to the back window.

I was afraid that someone might be in trouble.

I was especially afraid that it might be me.

Behind my cabin, down the slope of a ridge, something had erupted. But it wasn't a volcano. It was a herd of elk. A host of the animals covered the hill, descending in slow motion like a lava field with a thousand legs. The village of Mammoth was being invaded.

I started to rush outside. But I decided to dress first.

By the time I bolted out the front door, a pair of elk was meandering down the street, wandering at ease from cabin to cabin, bush to bush, sampling the shrubbery.

From behind the cabin, the moaning grew in volume and frequency. I was surrounded. Elk can be dangerous, I had read, so I heeded the encapsulated wisdom of the pamphlets and stayed on the front step of the cabin, ready to move inside at any provocation.

The imperturbable pair strolled down the street with the cool of a Fifties biker gang coming in to roust the locals. As they reached my cabin, I moved just inside the door. One of them stopped and munched a bush by my front window. She looked directly at me, as if waiting for an invitation to tea. When the request wasn't forthcoming, she soon moved on to other social opportunities. For wildlife, her manners were impeccable.

After the polite pair disappeared down the lane, I finished drying my hair and walked over to the nearby restaurant for my own dinner. From the outside, the building looked like a camp dormitory, but the interior was surprisingly elegant (surprising to me anyway). I don't remember everything I ordered. But I do recall the asparagus. I don't even like asparagus. But this was delicious and perfectly prepared: buttery and crisp and tender inside. More wilderness perfection.

By the time returned to my cabin, the elk had vanished into the fog. Only an occasional haunted wail proved that I hadn't been hallucinating.

In the cabin, I sat down at my laptop. I had still not written word one of my book. Occasionally at night, I would sit dutifully in front of the computer. But nothing arrived, even in the face of constant and overwhelming inspiration. I had even visited Inspiration Point. What more could I do?

But this time, when I turned on the laptop, something was wrong. The screen had turned a bright blue and the icons were almost invisible in the glare. Maybe bumping along the rough Yellowstone pavement had turned the brightness control, I thought. I knew what a brightness control looked like. I knew where the brightness control should be. I looked everywhere on the computer. I couldn't find the brightness control.

By squinting and holding the laptop just so in the light, I could still manage to read my email. But now any thought of writing a book on the journey was dashed. Somehow I dealt with the disappointment.

The next morning, Bernard and I once again went questing for moose. But again there were none to be found, so we continued south to the Norris Geyser Basin. About 15 miles south of

Mammoth Hot Springs, the basin sits at the middle of the figure eight of highway. There was no traffic jam this time, so in a few minutes we reached Norris.

If Yellowstone is Oz, then there must be witches, and you can see the cauldrons bubbling north, south, east, and west. More than 10,000 geothermal features can be found within the confines of Yellowstone.

Hot springs exist all through the park, extending into nearby areas like Chico. A hot spring works like this: Rain water sinks slowly through the porous rock at the surface and, after thousands of years, collects underground. The water is heated by the massive pool of magma that lurks deep under Yellowstone. Underground convection currents continuously exchange this superheated water with the colder liquid sinking down through the rocks. Eventually, the ancient boiling water seeps to the surface once more. At the surface, hot springs can form simple pools, limestone cones, or complex terraces like those at Mammoth Hot Springs.

Geysers work like hot springs, except that somewhere near the surface, a constriction exists that prevents the water from bubbling up normally. Pressure builds in the geysers until at some point the superheated water bursts through the constriction and erupts through to the surface. Geysers like Old Faithful are the most iconic feature of the park.

Mud pots are another geothermal feature abundant in Yellowstone. These are boiling pools of sulphuric acid mixed with melted rock; they bubble and toil and smell like rotten eggs.

Another form of hot spring, called steam vents or fumaroles, have more heat than water. The water boils off and escapes the ground as steam. You can see whole hillsides dotted with these vents, looking like a landscape from an episode of Star Trek.

The Norris basin is divided into two trails: Porcelain Basin and Back Basin. Porcelain Basin was visible from the parking lot, so that's where I headed first. Signs again warned that the crusty ground could give way at any moment, so once more I stayed on the boardwalks, circling the acres of open terrain. Blue-green bubbling pools dotted the barren landscape. Most of the pools were only a few yards wide, a fuming network linked by shallow streams meandering through the plateau. Steam drifted up off the pools in ghostly columns. A miniscule geyser frothed for a few seconds, then subsided.

I had almost completed the eerie circuit when I was met by another pair of quadrupeds, a mother and daughter, monitoring the path like park rangers making rounds. I suspected they were mule deer. But for Bernard's sake, I pretended they were moose.

Back Basin hosts a series of geysers, including Steamboat geyser, the largest in the park. It was getting pretty hot from the sun and the heat of the geysers and the lack of breeze. A woman in front of me nearly fainted and had to be helped to a bench. So I decided to stop and rest a bit on a wooden platform next to Echinus geyser.

The celebrated frequency of Old Faithful is unique. Most geysers are unpredictable. But at the time, Echinus eruptions were one of the more regular events. Since my visit, the geyser has reportedly become more unpredictable. But it's not my fault, I swear.

The pool around a geyser offers clues to the timing of the next eruption, so I leaned over the wooden railing and carefully observed the water around Echinus. The pool was almost full, the first sign of a pending eruption. Then the water started to bubble, another sign. Soon the pool began frothing, like the bubbles a kid makes blowing into his milk through a straw.

A baby spurt erupted from the center of the pool. Then another. Then a gush about a foot high, like a steaming water fountain for a thirsty giant. Then calmness for a second.

It was quiet.

Yeah.

Too quiet.

A column of water thick as a man exploded out of the pool. Like an enormous garden hose turned skyward, the gleaming pillar surged far above our heads, forty feet into the air, then splashed down into the billowing cloud of steam that had swallowed the now invisible pool. A mist blew back over the platform, warm as summer rain.

For two or three spectacular minutes, the geyser spouted and flared like an aqueous Roman candle, and the crowd around me on the platform thrilled to the show. Then Echinus subsided, devolving into an occasional mild percolation. Refreshed by the spectacle and mineral water shower, we departed Norris and headed east across the Yellowstone loop.

The problem with driving in Yellowstone, maybe one reason the roads are so bad, is this:

every mile or so, you have to stop to see something amazing. At the wolf meadow, the pup was again drawing a crowd, this time on the other side of the road. An experienced performer by now, marching to his own toy drummer, he ignored his audience to focus on the same serious game, creeping and pouncing, peeping and bouncing.

At the end of the crossroad, I turned down the southeastern side of the figure eight, avoiding the scary canyonlands. In a broad field by the lazy Yellowstone River, a large herd of buffalo posed in prehistoric effigy. I snuck up behind a stand of trees to get a better look. Through the tree in front of me, I saw something unusual: a flower about the size of a silver dollar. A black flower. A glossy black flower.

The flower stared at me.

The flower blinked.

The flower snorted.

The flower had black horns about six inches long and was moving in my direction, attached to a two thousand pound bison. I decided I had seen enough of flowers and ran (as fast as I could, trust me) to my car. On the website for Yellowstone, you can see a video of a bison effortlessly tossing a man into a tree. It looks like the same bison at the same tree. Just his little game I guess: Toss the Tourist.

I continued south to my next destination: Yellowstone Lake and the Lake lodge, built in the 1890s and extensively renovated in only 1903. As I sauntered through the hotel lobby, the aura of lost elegance haunted the whitewashed structure, as if a ghostly resort from the 1920s had risen on the lakeshore; the spirit of Gatsby would have felt right at home. Out the rear doors of a portico, I strolled over the lawn down to the shoreline.

An ocean on a mountaintop, Yellowstone Lake engulfed the horizon. Covering one hundred and thirty-six square miles and with an average depth of one hundred and forty feet, Yellowstone Lake is the largest high altitude lake in the US. Away on the eastern side, fifteen miles or more distant, snowy peaks poked their heads out of the hazy distance like prairie dogs out of a burrow. I sat on a rock by the lake, munched some peanut butter crackers, and tried to put the last two days into perspective.

So many times in Yellowstone, I felt as though my senses were deranged, seeing things that should not be: the river flowing backward; shrub-munching elks; wolf games; the lake on the mountain-top. The earth was unsteady, experience a hindrance, not a guide. I wasn't sure how much more disconcerting grandeur I could appreciate. So, to savor rather than dilute the experience, I decided to leave Yellowstone, and even I-90, behind.

But there was one more sight to see. I drove out from the lake and along the southern curve of the figure eight into a wasteland. The forest fires had been particularly devastating in this area, miles of hillsides decimated by the blaze, including Douglas firs five hundred years old. Signs of renewal were everywhere. But it looked as though decades, maybe centuries, would pass before the wasteland was fully healed.

About forty miles from the lake, I reached my destination: Old Faithful. Immediately, I felt on more familiar footing. The area is just as you have seen it in movies and National Geographic specials. Benches line the geyser perimeter and clocks are positioned to tell you when the next eruption is expected.

I had about ten minutes before the next event, so I explored the Old Faithful Inn, a massive log structure that stands next to the geyser area. At the gift shop, I bought a Coke (12 oz.) then walked outside and claimed a seat on a shadeless bench, enduring the bright afternoon sun. A crowd of maybe a hundred or so was ahead of me. But there was plenty of room, since the circle of benches sits well back from the geyser itself.

Only a minute or two delayed, Old Faithful started to erupt. I saw then why the benches were set back. A column of water far larger than Echinus launched up a hundred feet or more into the air, a towering crystalline willow. I had followed the retrograde river to the upside down waterfall.

A mist, lighter this time and cooler, anointed the surrounding sightseers, the spots on my glasses a small price to pay for history. After a few moments, Old Faithful was finished and so was I. I walked quickly out to the parking lot, cleaned my lenses, and began the drive south out of the park.

Yellowstone had one last joke for me. The Snake River flows south from Yellowstone past the park entrance, and the southern road follows the river. But the river descends a lot faster than the road. Soon I was again driving along a steep sloping chasm just waiting to swallow my car and me.

As the ravine got deeper, my driving got slower, until I had a long line of cars and trucks, big ones, behind me. I pulled over once to let the traffic out from behind me, but another line quickly formed, making me that much more nervous. Fortunately, I was driving on the inside lane rather than the outside. That's all that kept me going.

After twenty-some miles of serial breath-holding (much better than closing your eyes), I finally made it down and out of the mountains. I pulled over again to recover, which I always seemed to be doing in Yellowstone for one reason or another. The next time I go to Yellowstone, I'm bringing someone with me, someone who isn't afraid of heights. Or elk. Or wolves. Or buffalo. Or supervolcanos.

I got out of my car and wandered across a bridge, where a stream about forty feet wide joined the Snake. Upstream, I detected a loud rushing sound, so I hiked a bit through the trees and leaned out over some rocks to peer up the channel.

Maybe a hundred yards or so farther upstream, another waterfall splattered down, wide and not very high, but boisterous, unburdened, splashing along the rocky course. The air, full of spray and noise even so far downstream, felt fresh, untouched, healthy. I sat on a rock and closed my eyes and listened. Just remembering the sound:

*sssssshhhhhhhsssssshhhhhhhsssssshhhhhhsss
ssshhhhhhsssssshhhhhhhsssssshhhhhhssssss
hhhhhhhhsssshhhhhssssshhhhssssshhhhhhssssh
hhhsssssssshhhhssssssssshhhhhhhhhh*

puts me back there. I stayed for a time, to breathe and feel unburdened. It has become one of my peaceful places.

I knew by then the gifts in the Wizard's bag: two adult geysers and a baby geyser, two wolf pups (or the same wolf twice), pastel parapets, a hawk or osprey or eagle, boiling mudpots, nibbling elk, steaming vents, nosy mule deer, mountains, bison, valleys, squirrels, rivers, chipmunks, lakes, meadows, and waterfalls, waterfalls, waterfalls.

Even where there is no happiness, there is the next joy and the next.

The trick is to look.

Yellowstone taught me that. Home didn't look the same to Dorothy after Oz. But it was more beautiful, not less. Oz had taught her to see.

CHAPTER FIVE

Circles

Route 191 parallels the Grand Teton Range for about 40 miles, from Yellowstone to Jackson Lake. At every turn, an invisible hand lunges through your windshield and squeezes your lungs into an intake:

AAAAAAAAAAAAAHHHHHHHHHHH

or an expiration:

OOOOOOOOOOHHHHHHHHHHHHH

Snow-capped even in summer, the Grand Teton Mountains soar nearly 14,000 feet above sea level, looming more than a mile over the valley known as Jackson Hole. The Tetons are the youngest mountains in the US, born a mere ten million years ago. Like most youngsters, they are still growing, even as the floor of Jackson Hole sinks before them.

I had been traveling from mountain range to mountain range for my entire trip, each taller and more impressive than the last. The Catoctins of Maryland to the Blue Ridge of West Virginia. The Black Hills of South Dakota to the Absaroka of Yellowstone.

But the Tetons were the first mountains that truly looked the part, like the razor-edged fangs of gaping primeval jaws. Mile after mile, the Tetons dominated the surrounding land and sky with a preposterous immutable presence that dwarfed everything else.

As a species (homo sapiens sapiens—the wise wise humans), we have problems with perspective, demanding center stage in the universe and the hearts of the gods. We are learning, but neither our minds nor our language nor our institutions have caught up to our glimmering understanding. But in the presence of those towering peaks, perspective was easy.

There are seven billion humans in the world, roughly the same number I imagine as there are insects living on any one of the Teton mountains. If you put every human in the world together in one place (as we try to do each day on the Washington Beltway), we would all fit inside the confines of Yellowstone National Park, one corner of one state of one country of one world.

Scientists have catalogued about a million and a half species of animals on planet Earth. Estimates run as high as 49 million we don't yet know. Of those 50 million species, about 5000 are mammals (.01%). In the mammal category, although the human brain is the relative champ size-wise, the grey squirrel manages to remember the location of hundreds of nuts buried in a forest, while I have trouble finding my car keys. Of course, squirrels don't write books. Whether this puts them above humans or below, I can't quite work out.

In *Contact*, Jodie Foster (as astronomer Ellie Arroway) says:

> *You know, there are four hundred billion stars out there, just in our galaxy alone. If only one out of a million of those had planets, and just one out of a million of those had life, and just one out of a million of those had intelligent life; there would be literally millions of civilizations out there.*

I'm not sure I get the math there (four hundred billion divided by a million million million is pretty small). But I know what she is implying.

There are about 400 billion stars in our (rather small) galaxy. And there are maybe that many galaxies in the known universe (give or take a few billion), so that's 160 trillion billion stars (22 zeroes). And all those trillions of billions of stars account for only ten percent of the matter in the universe (90 percent is so-called dark matter), all of which occupies less than one percent of the volume of space in the universe. The rest is light.

The smallest structure in the universe, a quark, is about 10^{-16} meters in length. The known universe is 10^{26} meters wide. So the universe is 10^{42} times as big as a quark. That's 42 zeroes:

000000000000000000000000000000000000000000

Each of those zeroes represents a factor of ten. Of those 42 zeroes, the objects we evolved to sense (the ones we eat or that eat us) are in the range of about five zeroes, from a millimeter to maybe ten meters. That leaves 37 zeroes of ignorance.

We occupy a tiny part of a tiny part of one solar system, which is an incomprehensibly small part of the universe. If there is a plan for the universe, our species rates a footnote at best, and that most likely because we are mucking things up locally.

Late at night, when I can't stand any more talk shows or movies or sitcoms or news reports, I like to watch the NASA channel broadcasting pictures of earth sent back from space: white drifting over the blue, utterly peaceful, truly beautiful.

In the swirling serene complexity of water floating over floating water, the most beautiful spectacles are the most destructive: hurricanes. The Great Red Spot on the planet Jupiter, which has tantalized astronomers since Galileo, is a hurricane so massive it could swallow the Earth many times over. Our solar system is a hurricane of matter, our galaxy a hurricane of stars, our universe a hurricane of light. If a hurricane is beautiful from space, imagine the view from Eternity.

After just a few miles of Route 89, I was either hyperventilating or oxygen-depleted, I'm not sure which. Actually, I'm not sure there's a difference. So I pulled over at Jackson Lake.

Jackson Lake may well be the largest work of art in the world. From its headwaters in Yellowstone, the Snake River flows through Jackson

Hole, gathering itself at Jackson Lake before wending West and North through Oregon and Washington. In the early Twentieth century, Jackson Lake Dam was built at the south end of the lake, raising the water level some forty feet.

I found a comfortable place to sit by the lakeshore near the concrete wall of the dam. The broad motionless water mirrored the ice-capped peaks and the bold blue sky that framed them. After thousands of miles, I had finally found a manmade work that rivaled the splendor of nature. Of course, it did so by reflecting nature.

The glare of the sun, unrelenting on the immeasurable undulation of the lake surface, was hypnotic. I was tranquilized, meditation by mesmerization, absorbing and absorbed in perspective, my miniscule self echoed back to the vast expanse reflected at me, an exhilarating communion that laughed at otherness and extended beyond the bounds of my conscious self.

I had a nice time.

Eventually, despite my hypobaric euphoria, it occurred to me that I was hungry, so I left Jackson Lake and continued a few more miles to the town of Jackson, Wyoming. Jackson is a cowboy mall with a mountain range for a roof. The town had not yet geared up for the winter skiing season. But still I found a lively community of upscale hedonists that gloried in its frontier roots. There were more boot shops in Jackson than in all the other cities I have ever visited put together.

For the first time on my journey, I made a conscious decision to stay in the same place. Each day, I had moved on to new territory. I don't know why. Something just kept pushing me on. The unintentional effect was to pile experience on experience, to explore in a few hours what could easily take a week or a month or a lifetime.

Imagine visiting an art museum that contains only masterpieces. With each step, you enter another world. Each world is complete, complex, compelling. And each world heightens your senses for the next. There was no time to think, no will to write, because there was always something else to see or hear or feel, something else to wonder about or get excited by or stand in awe of. By the time I reached Jackson, I had also reached sensual intellectual emotional spiritual overload. Body and mind, heart and soul, needed a rest.

So in Jackson, for two days and two nights, I slept or watched TV or read the local newspaper, venturing out at odd hours only to the restaurant next door. I wasn't looking for action in Jackson, but the reverse.

In a creative process, there is a time when the conscious mind is set aside—tricked or distracted or even sedated. That's when the real work of writing begins in the unconscious, or wherever it happens—I don't claim to know. Writing to me is listening. Editing is listening closer. Just don't ask me what I'm listening to.

Though I didn't know it at the time, that's what Jackson was for me, a time to absorb, to fix in the blood, solve et coagula. I know I missed a lot in Jackson. But metamorphosis requires repose. Jackson was my cocoon.

After two days of indoor life, of reruns and snack food and the Wyoming Tribune-Eagle, I launched outdoors again with a renewed energy. But I soon faced another consequence of my plan to not plan: the constant need to make decisions.

When I started the journey, I had a vague direction: West to Yellowstone. When I left Jackson, I was truly wandering.

When you have no idea where you are going, there's no way to plan how to get there. Each intersection becomes a decision, each attraction a distraction. Making up your mind at 75 miles an hour is not a deliberative process. Indecision becomes decision. That's when I got lost.

A few miles south of Jackson, Route 191/89 splits. Route 191 goes east. Route 89 goes west. I intended to take 191, but somehow I got on 89 instead. So for quite a while, none of what I was seeing on the road was matching up with my map.

Eventually, I tossed the map into the back seat and just followed my instincts. Because it really didn't matter where I was, or where I was going, or when I got there. If the road was good and the drive was interesting, that was enough. I figured that sometime I'd encounter something big enough to tell me where I was.

And somehow, life outside mirrored life inside, but like a mirror, backward. I got lost as I found myself. Or in finding myself I got lost. Or maybe I found myself because I was lost. Some say it's the destination. Some say it's the journey. The view depends on your point. But it was all one to me then.

From Jackson, Wyoming, to Logan, Utah, Route 89 wanders around through national forests: Targhee first, then Caribou, then a long way through Bridger-Teton running the Salt River Range, and then finally Cache National Forest.

The drive—okay call it a meandering—from Jackson to Logan was as delightful and mellow as any part of my trip.

Miniature splendors emerged along the route. Smoke plumes spired over farmhouse flues. Veils of mist crept down from the hills to cloak the homesteads. Horses in concert paced in pastures with whitewashed fences, or congregated in corners to swap the equine gossip of day. Intense fall splatters of reds and oranges highlighted the high country. I wasn't in awe or astonished or stunned or amazed. I was entranced.

Staying on 89, I drifted briefly into Idaho, then circled around east again on Route 30, crossing into the northern tip of Utah. I think. I really was lost, until I drove out of the hills directly at and almost into a massive body of water.

Twenty miles long, eight miles wide, and almost 6000 feet above sea level, Bear Lake shares its bounty across the border between Idaho and Utah. Bits of limestone suspended in the water create an unusual turquoise color (though this wasn't as noticeable when I was there because of the overcast sky.)

Bear Lake was a shock. I just couldn't get used to finding sealets in the mountains. God's exterior decorator had some more explaining to do.

Past Bear Lake on 89, I entered Logan Canyon. I don't know who Logan was, but he makes a fine canyon. The highway runs alongside a creek maybe ten feet wide, which on that day was no more than a persistent trickle. Yet the relentless flow had carved a ravine hundreds of feet deep.

My own flow was not relentless but aimless, not creating a path but taking the one tendered under the watchful protection of the Wasatch mountain range. But once I reached Ogden, Utah, I had located myself again. I was expecting the Great Salt Lake, so I wasn't surprised when I saw it, though it was another huge body of water where there shouldn't be one.

The Great Salt Lake is enormous, but it is only a remnant of a much larger prehistoric body of water known as Lake Bonneville (same as the salt flats). This prehistoric inland sea once covered 20,000 square miles from Logan to Provo. Thousands of years ago the lake disappeared in an enormous flood. Has anyone searched for Noah's Ark in Utah?

Salt sea on one side of me, mountains on the other, I passed the western edge of Salt Lake City then zipped onto I-80, another major east-west interstate that runs along the south end of the lake. After about five miles, I pulled across the road into at a gas station, facing east, and spread the map out across the steering wheel. I had a decision to make.

In the afternoon sun, the air simmered off the pavement around me. In the rear-view mirror, the flat arid expanse of western Utah shimmered. Through the windshield, I could just make out the purple outline of the mountains to the east.

I had no reason to go home. No one was expecting me, or even waiting for me. I had no job, no wife, no kids. Nothing substantial about my life had changed. And I had been feeling so unburdened after Jackson. I loved the road just flowing under my wheels. Wherever. Whatever.

There were some practical considerations. I-80 runs through Nevada to Reno in the northwest end of the state. Between Salt Lake City and Reno, there didn't appear to be much but desert and it would have taken me far into the night to reach Reno. This would have broken my unspoken rule of stopping before nightfall.

But stronger than everything else I had an intuition I couldn't explain: I had gone as far as I needed to, maybe, as far as I was supposed to.

I pulled out of the gas station and headed east. Not home yet. But east.

When I got back to Salt Lake City, I turned south on Route 15 and spent the night in Provo. At the motel, I picked up my usual set of brochures (though the rack was rather paltry) and found one for Sundance, Robert Redford's ski resort. The resort, just a few miles outside Provo, sits nestled in a cleft of the mountains.

I had always thought of Utah as a desert state, yet my entire passage so far had been into, over, or alongside of mountains. Even though I knew Utah was famous for skiing, I never pictured it so mountainous. Had I thought about it, I'm fairly sure I would have deduced that very few people enjoy skiing in the desert.

The next day I drove out to Sundance, an easy non-scary mountain drive from Provo, for which I was thankful. There was no snow in the mountains (for which I was also thankful), yet there were quite a few people at the resort. Sundance offers a range of non-winter activities like hiking, mountain biking, a day camp for kids, a summer theater program, and the ever-popular celebrity watch.

The resort was set up in a campus-like arrangement, an eclectic collection of structures arranged in a laid-back atmosphere with no hint of its glamorous Hollywood pedigree. In keeping with the relaxed feel, I took my lemonade (no coke this time) outside to quest covertly for signs of movie stars. It was a beautiful day in a spectacular setting, so I wasn't too disappointed that I didn't recognize anyone.

Leaving Sundance, I zagged southeast, cutting across Utah on smaller roads (as I have mentioned, I don't always learn my lesson the first time). I had absolutely no idea where I was going, and didn't even look at a map this time. I still hadn't made a decision to head home. But I was tending eastward.

After several hours wandering through scenic eastern Utah, I caught up with I-70, yet another one of those major east-west interstates. I-70 did not have for me the caché of I-90, so I briefly considered continuing south to Lake Powell, another huge manmade lake that straddles the Utah-Arizona border. But something kept me heading east. I-70 was going my way.

I was out of the Utah mountains and the verdant areas surrounding them and finally encountered an arid expanse that matched my preconceptions. The area was the ancient homeland of a tribe called the Anasazi, who mysteriously disappeared from the area long before the post-Columbus arrival of the Spanish. On the canyon walls, the Anasazi left pictographs resembling (among other things) tall thin bipeds in space helmets. I had finally located my aliens.

After several hours of driving, a line of mesas appeared in the distance like colored ribbons stacked in layers. The tall sharp-edged ridge seemed to go on as far as I could see.

The Book Cliffs are a rugged rock wall 1000 feet high and 200 miles long, the longest unbroken escarpment in the world. Yet I had never heard of them. How could someone who loved books as much as I do never have heard of the Book Cliffs? How could I not be aware of such massive and extraordinary formations? How could I keep being surprised at being surprised?

The Book Cliffs continued to disabuse my ignorance as I passed from Utah into Colorado. The terrain was striking, flat and arid, not quite desert but not far from it. This was not at all the way I pictured Colorado, which was supposed to be elevated and snowy with lots of beer. Once more, my picture of the world needed adjustment.

I spent the night in Grand Junction, Colorado. I had no idea what Grand Junction joined. But I liked the sound of it. After dinner I strolled outside to see what the stars looked like from the

Colorado desert. Two annoying moons flooded the parking lot with electric pink illumination, so I ventured around the corner of the building and found a nice dark spot. It was hazy that night, but I could still see countless stars suspended in the De Profundis sky.

Light propagates in waves (there's a joke there somewhere). The frequency of a light wave—the distance from one peak to another (another joke: I'll just point them out when I find them)—can range from unimaginably small gamma rays to radio waves with frequencies a kilometer or longer.

Only certain frequencies of light can be detected by the human eye. The visible colors from red to violet have wavelengths ranging from 700 to 400 nanometers (a billionth of a meter). There's a reason for that; these are the primary frequencies that can pass through the Earth's atmosphere (except for radio waves, which have frequencies much larger than the human eye and can't be seen).

So of all the information passing through the universe in the form of electromagnetic radiation, we evolved to perceive and process only a fragment. Until recently, our capacity for sensing that universe has been hugely limited by a design process that favored survival over understanding.

The closest star to Earth is Proxima Centauri, part of the Centaurus constellation. This stellar assembly, now visible chiefly south of the equator thanks to the astronomical process known as precession, was once visible to the Greeks.

Centaurus was named after Chiron, in Greek mythology the wise and immortal centaur (half-human, half horse) who was a physician and the tutor of the demigods. A young Hercules accidentally wounded Chiron and even the legendary healer could not cure himself of this wound. His suffering was so terrible, Chiron decided to renounce his immortal heritage and die. Zeus, the Divine Monarch of the Greek pantheon, affixed Chiron's image in the stars forever.

Men have imagined pictures in the stars at least as long as 4000 years ago, and probably much longer. The Sumerians divided the sky into twelve arcs, called the Zodiac. This system was passed along by the Chaldeans, who were also said to be exceptional astronomers.

Constellations (and astrology, the practice of prediction based on the Zodiac) are a fascinating example of a belief overtaken by science. That hasn't slowed its practice; almost every local newspaper I read across the country had a column of horoscopes, and I read almost every one.

But the stars in a constellation only appear to be near one another. Proxima Centauri, the brightest star in the Centaur constellation, is four light years away from earth. Beta Centauri, another star in the constellation, is three hundred light years away.

A light year is the distance that a beam of light travels in one year (scientists, mental travelers, also find it easier to talk in time instead of miles). That comes to about six trillion miles (twelve zeroes). Four light years then is 24 trillion miles. Since leaving home, I had driven 4000 miles in 20 days: 200 miles per day, or 73000 miles per year. At that rate, I would reach Proxima Centauri in about 329 million years, assuming non-rush hour traffic.

The farthest known object in the universe is a quasar, about 14 billion light years (or 90 billion trillion miles) away. At my Cavalier pace, I could reach a quasar in one million billion years, thousands of times longer than the universe has existed.

The Sumerians and Chaldeans, drawing pictures in the sky, tried their best to make sense of a universe they did not have the tools to understand. I admire that impulse. But given the choice, I would rather think that I don't know than think that I know what I don't. If God gave us a mind to understand, to believe or disbelieve is to reject the gift.

Astrophysicists have a theory called the Anthropic principle. This principle has two flavors: Strong and Weak.

The Strong Anthropic principle states that only what is observed exists. I use a financial corollary of this theory: If I don't open my mail, I won't have to pay my bills.

The Weak Anthropic principle is more clever and more intriguing. According to this theory, the universe is the way it is because it is the way it has to be to produce an entity that is capable of asking why the universe is the way it is. In other words, because we are around to ask questions, we can deduce that the universe must have those characteristics common to universes with people who ask questions. The unquestioning universe would undoubtedly be more peaceful. But it would likely have no mountains.

Humans like to hold themselves apart from nature. Man was made in the image of God. Man possesses an eternal soul. Man is the only animal who blushes, or needs to. But if there is any distinguishing human characteristic, I think it is our need for meaning. Man is the animal who means.

We are engineered to find meaning wherever we look; our search for significance has no bounds and one end. We attach meaning to anything and everything that we perceive or experience. And meaning is always for us, about us. Revelation is our real daily bread.

Humans find meaning in patterns, in connecting the dots. Yet as we are slowly realizing, the dots aren't what we used to think they were. Ordinary language is mapped to the operation of the human mind. Just as the mind can't comprehend the truth, ordinary language (discursive, discrete, fact-based names and word patterns) can't express the truth. So we are poorly equipped for celestial dictation.

The impulse is right. God would speak in horizons. He would paint pictures in the stars. But the flesh is weak.

We are the creature that means. We need meaning. So we accept whatever mythos we can scratch or juggle out of the elements. Like the ancient astrologers, we connect the stars in the sky, when those stars in fact have no relation to one another except the one we provide. Or if there is a connection, it is beyond human knowing until the true Grand Junction.

We long for a personal revelation. Emerson insisted on it. But for now, revelation is incomplete, a dim suggestion, through a glass darkly, a puppet show on the wall of a cave. The fact is, our minds are designed for facts, not truth. The truth of the universe is beyond our grasp, though we may occasionally get a sneak senseless peek among the peaks.

And meaning in the universal sense, the sense that our lives are part of a grand scheme, Purpose with a Capital P, must grow from truth. There may be no meaning in the truth of the world. Or if there is, it may not be meaning for us. The truths we hold self-evident are neither self-evident nor true.

We are the animal that means. In that capacity lies responsibility. I have a theory, which I call my Anthropomorphic theory. This theory also comes in two versions: Weak and Strong.

In the Weak version of my Anthropomorphic theory, we learn to live in a world where meaning is unattainable and sense is contingent nonsense. This version puts us ahead of all of those people who don't know they don't know. But it doesn't help us decide how to save the world or what to have for breakfast.

In the Strong version of my Anthropomorphic theory, the universe appears without meaning so we can create meaning. The mystery of the universe is a gift. The mystery of life is a revelation.

Everything we know is wrong, everything we believe is flawed, because the language in which we think and believe is inadequate to express the truth. But mark my words: expression precedes understanding.

Love a poet. Buy his pencils. Buy him pencils. Language is newborn in the age of the world and new born every day. And after only a few thousand years, we have Emily. And Will. And Waldo.

We have two goals: first, to find the truth; second, to live as best we can until we do. What we can conceive cannot be separated from what we can express. How we live cannot be separated from what we can discover. As we step forward to collective independence and make a path sacred to ourselves, the essential human choices are breakfast and poetry.

In stretching ourselves, in taking responsibility for our values, in claiming our Categorical independence, we set ourselves on the path to create the language that can express and the mind that can comprehend whatever ultimate truth we can eventually discover. Then maybe someone will tell us what is going on. They (God or the aliens or whoever) could be waiting for us.

Turns out that Grand Junction is where the Gunnison River joins the Colorado.

So.

Okay.

I was hoping for more.

The following morning, I left my disjunction at Grand Junction behind. Tracking the Colorado River up I-70, I passed De Beque (possibly named for a character in South Pacific), Parachute (possibly named for an air safety device), and Rifle (possibly named for the long firearms I imagined pointing at me). I had never heard of any of them. If I-90 was The Road Not Taken, I-70 was The Road Not Known.

Glenwood Springs is a cozy Colorado town at the foot of the mountains and Denny's restaurant was the after-church place to see and be seen. As I sat in my booth reading the Sunday Denver

Post, I watched family after family flock to the crowded restaurant and line up outside in their Sunday best, waiting for a place at the table. For a man who had driven four thousand solitary miles, the sight of families going out to breakfast after church was wistfully delightful. But for the first time on my trip, I felt alone.

After breakfast, I turned off I-70 and headed up into the mountains. I do mean up. Why was everything I wanted to see in the mountains? As I ascended into the heights, other patterns in my journey began to emerge, like dots awaiting connection.

Monuments.

Paths.

Hawks.

Waterfalls.

Stars.

I was wandering. Just wandering. Unplanned. Haphazard. Yet somehow the random elements of the journey had begun to form patterns. Even the Emerson that I read at night seemed somehow in concert with my exploits during the day. It almost seemed as if the journey was shaping itself, showing me what it wanted me to see. Or was that what I wanted to see? Or was that in truth my work?

The town of Aspen, Colorado, made my heart go pitter-pat and it wasn't just the altitude (about 9000 feet above sea level). Aspen is Boomer Valhalla, where we go when we die or get rich, whichever comes first.

I nosed my Cavalier through the crowded streets, experiencing a near-religious ecstasy. On every street corner, an upscale saloon gathered in the pilgrims while the coffee house confessional next door sanctified the faithful. I savored the mountainous wealth and rustic je ne sais quoi of the star-struck community. But I didn't stop. When I reached the town limits, I kept on going. I left Aspen for aspen.

The city of Aspen is named for the trees. Of course. You knew that. I never thought about it until I drove out of town.

An aspen grove is one of the largest known living creatures. Aspen reproduce through a process called root suckering, a kind of cloning in which a parent tree generates a vast underground complex of roots. Some of these roots shoot up through the soil, sprouting into what appears to be a new aspen tree. But in reality the new tree is just an appendage of the parent, genetically identical and connected invisibly by interlinked roots.

An entire grove of aspen can be considered one organism. A single grove in the Wasatch mountains covers 200 acres and is estimated to weigh more than 500 tons.

Leaving town to the east, aspen lined both sides of the road. The aspen is a deciduous tree and in autumn, which comes early at that altitude, the leaves turn color before they fall away. The foliage in Aspen that late September was probably a few days past its vivid peak.

But in the afternoon sun, the suspended leaves burned brilliant in the sunlight, glowing saffron and swaying in the breeze like Japanese lanterns. The lustrous foliage transmuted the two-lane road out of town into a golden highway, as numberless slender trunks, bunched together in rooted solidarity, lined the way like pillars of amber. It was Tolkien's fantasy come to life, Laurelindorenan, Land of the Valley of Singing Gold.

So enchanting was that close-set grove that I didn't notice that the road was going up. Rapidly. If you look at the map, the eastern and western roads out of Aspen look much the same. In reality, the western road is a broad highway that climbs gently though relatively flat land. Airport type land. House building land. The eastern road, on the other hand, is a narrow two-lane cart path that dangles for miles on the edge of a cliff. For much of the year, the road is closed because travel is too dangerous.

On my right, the ravine was sinking deeper and deeper and nothing but a hypnotic yellow corridor of aspen shielded me from the sheer and steepening chasm. Then the aspen stopped and adrenaline rushed in.

To make things perilously worse, I was on the OUTSIDE lane this time. Any error would plunge my car over the cliff. Like radar, my eyes tracked each passing car, accompanied by a string of exclamations in ascending perfect pitch:

Oh God!
Oh God!!
Oh God!!!
Whew.
Oh God!
Oh God!!
Oh God!!!
Whew.

My car began going slower and slower, of its own volition I suppose, since I have no memory of actively driving. Yes, I was the one, the slow driving idiot that Sunday outside Aspen. As the line of cars behind me began growing longer and longer, I looked for a place to pull off or turn around. To no avail. On the left was steep rock wall. On the right was doom. I had to keep going.

Then, half a mile up ahead, rounding a curve in the road, I saw it. My fingers blanched on the wheel like trees taking root, as the blood drained from extremities like my brain. I grew light-headed, just the thing to reassure you when you're driving on a cliff. I heard a long siren alternating between cursing and prayer. I realized it was my own voice.

The Terror was closer.

Just a few hundred yards away.

Monstrous and lumbering.

Relentless and deadly.

A Recreational Vehicle.

Forty feet long and twenty feet wide, a mansion on wheels was careening toward me on a two-lane mountain road. It was dead ahead; and just then I understood the origin of that phrase. With the superior vision granted the dying, I could just make out the faces of the couple sitting up front.

A man and a woman.

White-haired.

Smiling.

Retirees.

Maniacs.

RV drivers.

They looked so happy, perched in their comfy captain's chairs. I was not happy. Frantically, my eyes darted from cliff to road to empty space. No way to turn back. Then the insane drivers behind me began passing me on the left. I was trapped like a mammoth down a sinkhole.

The Recreational Behemoth dieselled around the final curve, half of the vehicle overhanging oblivion. Then it hit the straightaway and began to pick up speed. I was cool under fire:

You madman! You madman!
I'm going over! I'm going over!
Oh God!
Oh God!!
Oh God!!!

Whew.

With room to spare, the RV passed me by.

Of course.

You knew that.

In shocked relief, I managed to make it the rest of the way up the mountain. I turned off the road and parked. I tried taking my pulse, but I kept losing count. I took long deep breaths. But I was ON TOP OF A MOUNTAIN at the time, so it didn't help.

Not far from where I had parked, I spotted a sign:

> *Independence Pass*
> *Elevation 12,095 Feet*
> *Continental Divide*

I had never stood on higher ground.

To the north, a broad bank of brilliant aspen topped a ridge, shocking yellow against blue-white sky. To the south and west, the golden valley stretched away. To the east, a crowd had gathered. At first, I thought they had been watching me drive up the pass. But they were facing away from me off an overlook of some sort.

I had ascended two miles high into the mountains, risking life and limb and sanity. What Oracle would speak to me? What Guru would enlighten me? What Revelation would be granted me?

Bernard urged me on. I pushed through the crowd, threading my way past those who had preceded me to the edge. Grasping the railing, I peered out from the top of Independence Pass. There were no words for what I saw. No words. So instead, out loud, I laughed.

I saw mountains. Mountains as far as I could see. Mountains everywhere. All mountains. Nothing but mountains.

I looked up to the bright blue heavens and whispered in honest appreciation:

Very Funny.

Back down by the car, Bernard posed on the sign for Independence Pass. I stepped back to take a picture. How cute, said a girl. Buddha smiles, was my thought.

*
*
*

I drove between mountains. Around mountains. Over mountains. I passed Mount Elbert (at 14,443 feet, the highest peak in Colorado), Twin Lakes (though mountain lakes no longer surprised me), Leadville (a historic mining town), until by evening I arrived back at I-70, and Vail.

Vail, Colorado, is built up the slope of a mountainside in a picturesque but labyrinthine layout of one-way streets and places you can see but not get to. Everyone in Vail must own a helicopter because that's the only way I can see of getting from one end of the town to the other.

I spent the night at the Marriott Resort at the western end of town. My suite cost only $25 dollars a night. I don't know why. Maybe I looked desperate for respite.

When I awoke the next morning, someone had stolen the oxygen. Vail is 9000 feet above sea level and the altitude was finally getting to me—my asthma (miasma?) didn't help. So I jumped in my car, followed my trail of breadcrumbs to escape the maze (sorry about mixing my mythology) and began my descent from the mountaintop.

A few hours down I-70, I stopped at an overlook at the end of the mountains and the beginning of Denver, Colorado. Denver that day had smog a mile high and was no place for the asthmatic. So I turned north to Boulder.

Founded at the foot of the Rockies, Boulder, Colorado, is a postmodern Elysium with the University of Colorado as its center of gravitas. I wandered a while around the university campus, hoping to absorb some inspiration. I still had not written a creative word on the trip. And since my laptop malfunction, I had pretty much even given up on email.

I was inspired, but not write. I sat on a brick wall and just watched everything whirl around me. The campus seemed like an alien world (not that I'm admitting to visiting any), consistently paradoxical yet vaguely familiar:

No one did anything.

Yet everyone seemed preoccupied.

The air was filled with energy.

But nothing ever happened.

No one spoke.

All communication was by Frisbee.

In this land, our forefathers pioneered a delicate miracle, a social system that promotes the individual and permits the solitary quest for truth. Our universities are the symbol of that gift, and sometimes its location or means.

The freedom to pursue your own truth, along with the understanding that there is truth yet to pursue, is our gift to ourselves. In all of human history, it is very rare. We need to protect the gift at all costs, except the cost of the gift itself.

Sitting on a stone wall on the campus in Boulder, at the base of the Rocky Mountains, I naturally (for me anyway) thought of Sisyphus. In Greek Mythology, King Sisyphus betrayed the Gods in some manner (accounts vary). For his crime, he was condemned after death to roll a massive boulder up a mountainside for all eternity. As soon as he neared the top, the boulder would slip from his grasp and tumble back to the bottom. I was making my own descent.

That night I settled in my hotel room, opened my copy of Emerson to the essay *Circles*, and read the first paragraph. Then I closed the book and put it away.

Leaving Boulder the following morning, I had another decision to make. I could head northeast on Route 76 and catch I-80 in Nebraska. Or I could continue along I-70. I-80 would take me back through Iowa, where my father was born. I had been to Iowa a few times, and had relatives there. I wanted to maintain that fresh mountain isolation, which meant avoiding reality for a while longer. So I decided instead to continue east on I-70.

In retrospect, Iowa would have been the better choice. Avoiding reality isn't realistic.

Colorado is another mixed-up state, with desert in the west, mountains in the middle, and plains in the east. I made good time on I-70 through the flat eastern terrain, entering Kansas by late morning. About 100 miles into Dorothy's home state, I was in the left lane of two, on cruise control at the speed limit as was my habit. Very few cars were on the road.

In my rear view mirror, I saw a Kansas State Trooper racing up behind me, traveling much faster than my 75 miles per hour. Figuring it was an emergency of some sort, I quickly pulled into the right lane to get out of his way. He zipped behind me, flashed his lights, and pulled me over. His reason: not using my turn signal to change lanes. I thought then and think now that it was a dirty trick. I was the victim of Easterner profiling or Cavalier profiling or White Bearded Guy profiling.

The trooper approached my car from the passenger's side. He looked about thirty years old, clean cut and trim. Fortunately, Bernard had jumped into my knapsack at the last stop, so I didn't have to worry about that particular embarrassment. I rolled down the passenger window. The trooper nodded politely. In a practiced, professional, pseudo-friendly voice, he asked me if I was carrying any drugs or guns.

I didn't answer for a moment, not because I was carrying any drugs or guns, but because no one had ever asked me that before. After a second, I said no in a truthful though puzzled voice, wondering why he was asking and whether anyone actually said yes. He explained that I-70 was a major route for drug running out of Denver. Then he asked me what I was doing.

Again I didn't answer for a moment. I was stumped. Was there a word for what I was doing? What was I doing? How could I explain it? I could tell him I was on vacation. I could tell him about my divorce and how I quit my job. I could tell him how I was wandering the country trying to write a book that I couldn't seem to start...

I would never make it on a game show. The tangents would do me in. After a long few seconds of earnest cogitation, I sputtered a bit. Then I said I was just driving around. In hindsight, I could have said I was on a transcendental pilgrimage to sacred sites in the heartland of America that was transforming my vision of the universe. But I think he would have asked to look in the trunk anyway.

As I got out of the car to open the trunk, I started to get worried. I was alone on a nearly deserted highway with a state trooper who suspected I was armed and running drugs. No one knew where I was. I wondered: Do they take Visa in prison?

I popped the lid to my trunk. My Cavalier was a fantastic little car, but it didn't have much trunk room. Mine was packed…no that sounds too neat. My trunk was chaos come to Kansas, stuffed to the latch with clothes and books and vegetarian junk food and books and mementos and books and my defunctive laptop.

Something in the mess must have convinced the officer that I wasn't a threat to society. I like to think it was the box of books on quantum physics, because then bringing them wasn't a complete waste of space-time. Anyway, he gave me a warning about signaling lane changes and then let me go.

When I was on the road again, I got pretty upset, in the way you get upset after something bad has happened and not during it. I'm not in

Kansas anymore and I don't think I'm going back (at least not without a reprieve from the Governor). Huffing like a fumarole, I hurled down the highway, determined to escape from Kansas before nightfall. I had paranoid visions of being tracked by helicopter until I ratted on my supplier. Since I didn't have a supplier, it would have been a long flight.

It may seem like I'm whining a lot over a warning, especially to those people who are stopped routinely because of their accent or the color of their skin. But the encounter brought me back to what I'd spent weeks (months? years?) trying to avoid: real life.

My journey so far had been spectacular in the truest sense, the adventures invigorating, the freedom intoxicating (maybe the officer smelled freedom on my breath). But Kansas was a rude reintroduction to the real world with real people and real problems. Like me and mine. When she returned to Kansas, Dorothy had her family and friends around her. I was alone.

In 1833, Emerson returned from his voyage to Europe. By 1836, he had married again, moved to Concord, published *Nature*, and celebrated the birth of his son Waldo. I was now just a couple of days from home, and that brought up many uncomfortable questions:

What had I been through? What did it mean? How was I different? Was I different?

And what now? And how? And where? And with whom?

I had to begin my life again. But I had no answers.

Kansas is a long state and I had a lot of time to brood while driving in the right lane and keeping an eye out for the Feds. How do we act in a world we have not evolved to comprehend? What values do we live by once we suspect that our inherited rules are the byproducts of unenlightened processes? Where is the answer to where is the answer?

After uncounted hours and miles of pensive preoccupation, I spotted a billboard. Set back a bit from the road, the sign was for the Russell-Stover candy factory. Immediately my mind was flooded with memories.

My grandmother's name was Daisy. Sometime in the Sixties, a blood vessel burst behind her optic nerve and she went almost entirely blind. I became her seeing-eye kid. On game days, we would sit together listening to Washington Senator's baseball games on radio, consoling ourselves for the inevitable loss with the oval delights of Russell-Stover chocolates. She always had a stash, because her beau (as she called him) would send for her birthday or holiday or just whenever boxes of assorted candies.

And when I saw that billboard, suffused in childhood memories, I suddenly felt sure that everything was all right. The abrupt change of mood was astonishing to say the least. Maybe it was the proximity to that much chocolate. That my sign from the universe was an actual sign only made it better. Buddha smiles.

I got as far as Lawrence on the eastern side of Kansas before stopping for the night. By late the next morning, I had reached Missouri, once again headed east on I-70. But this time, I knew, I was heading home.

As I drove around Kansas City, other memories flooded in. I had flown out from Washington to Kansas City (the Missouri side) where I saw the first professional production of my first play. I felt like a celebrity. I felt like a writer.

But I didn't stop in Kansas City, or anywhere else in Missouri. I tracked across the state in a day, circled around Saint Louis, and took I-64 to southern Indiana. At dusk, I pulled into a motel in my namesake Evansville and parked in a lot next to a cornfield. For a moment, the plummeting sun was suspended over the field, colossal and fusion-orange. Then it plunged below view, setting the silhouetted corn ablaze. I sat on the hood of my car, leaning against the windshield, and watched until darkness.

I-64 crossed the Ohio River at Louisville and passed on through Kentucky, and the next day so did I. The trees sported fall fashions in a dramatic show. I had eyes like a hawk, always engorged, always famished. Genius is the inability to not see. In Kentucky, I was a genius of leaves.

I-64 threads through Lexington, then twists slightly northeast toward West Virginia. Midway, a butterfly dipped in front of my car. The driver-side windshield wiper caught one of his wings and he was trapped.

I was traveling through a ravine at the time and there was nowhere to pull off. I slowed as much as I could to lessen the wind damage, but his free wing was buffeted viciously by the driven air. After several horrifying minutes, I finally came to a truck stop and pulled off the road. The car rumbled to a standstill on the gravel, and I jumped out, hoping the butterfly was still alive.

I didn't recognize the species, but she was large, about the size of a Monarch. Her shiny black wings were marked by brilliant blue spots of various sizes, almost Missouri Blue. I wondered whether she had been migrating to her breeding ground. Some species I knew traveled thousands of miles to mate.

I gently disentangled the wing from the wiper blade and set her on the hood. She kept flipping her right wing, but her left was ripped and useless. The wing that had been trapped was broken, not the wing that was free in the wind.

The slope behind the truck stop was thickly wooded with a small grassy strip in front. Not knowing what else to do, I ripped a blank piece of paper from a notebook and coaxed the butterfly onto it. Then I gently laid her in the grass by the woods.

Forsaking her broken wing, the butterfly moved away with a measured delicate motion, slow painstaking meticulous placement of the foot in each tentative step on her newfound earthbound path. After a few moments, weeks maybe in butterfly time, she disappeared into the brush.

As I continued down I-64, I recalled the words that had fluttered into my head on the way to Pipestone: Death by Butterfly Wings. Then I heard more words about the butterfly in my head. Well, not the butterfly in my head. Well, maybe the butterfly in my head. I repeated the verse into my little silver tape recorder, which was again operating normally:

> *Butterfly with a broken wing,*
> *why were you made so delicate?*
> *It is your wings now that keep you from walking.*
> *Take them off and walk*
> *into the long grass and be quiet.*
> *Walk into the tall quiet grass*
> *and lay your eggs. Seed the future.*
> *How can those tiny wings carry*
> *the beauty of the world? Let them go.*
> *Butterfly with a broken wing,*
> *there is nothing I can do for you*
> *but remember.*

After I finished, I played the tape back over and over, astonished and grateful. I had written something, put words together creatively, for the first time in years. Maybe it wasn't brilliant, but for Interstate Poetry it wasn't bad.

In shock at my near-writing experience, I careened (sorry, I'm just tired of saying drove) through the rest of Kentucky, wound up and down and around and through the familiar mountains of West Virginia, until finally stopping near the Virginia border. It was late and the night was so dark I could hardly find my way to the Greenbrier.

The Greenbrier is a famous resort in White Sulphur Springs, West Virginia, a haven for Presidents, the mindlessly wealthy, and people who don't like driving in the dark. The grounds are stunning, with meticulously tended golf courses, manicured pastures and sparkling brooks, and the colonnaded architecture of the Old South, all framed then by the kaleidoscopic autumn display of mountain forests. Or so they say. It was too dark to see any of it.

My room that night cost nearly twenty times as much as my suite in Vail (and that a discount rate because I arrived so late). But I said okay. It was the last night of my journey. Some antebellum celebration was called for.

I was too tired to go down for dinner, so I called room service (the one place on my trip where I had that luxury). They said my dinner would arrive in forty-five minutes, so I showered and relaxed, and browsed through the hotel reading material. Then I noticed a writing desk.

I opened my laptop on the desk, set Bernard on one side and the Pipestone turtle on the other, then spent several minutes arranging the desk lamp. Squinting just so, I began to write nearly invisible words on the blue white screen. It wasn't email. It wasn't even the book I had intended to write. It was a play.

Years before, I had written the first three pages of a play. I hadn't touched it, had barely thought of it, in nearly a decade. For some reason that night the words started to flow. And wouldn't stop. A dialogue between a scientist and an angel. Set in a casino. Spirituality. Quantum physics. Slot machines. A blockbuster for sure.

It wasn't my Carl Sagan book. I didn't care. I was writing again.

Pages poured out of me. When my dinner was delivered, I munched between punch lines. A little after midnight, I finished the first act. One entire act of a play in one session, from a man who had hardly written a page in almost a decade. That was a miracle.

I gently closed the laptop and went down to the bar to celebrate. A live band of six pieces or so was playing old pop standards: Cole Porter and such. A few couples danced in the intimate dim. Alone at the deep-burnished mahogany bar, I perched on a stool, murmured with the music, and saluted my finale with champagne. Every end is a Beguinning.

Even breakfast in the Greenbrier dining room is semi-formal, so the next morning I staggered groggily out to my car to locate my blazer and tie. I hadn't seen either since about Wisconsin. I finally unearthed them (literally), stuffed between my box of books and a hunk of 60 million year old fossilized driftwood I had bought as a souvenir in South Dakota

I donned them in the parking lot (a faux pas perhaps) and proceeded to the grand dining room, where the waiters were all much better dressed than I was. In spite of that, I thoroughly enjoyed an exquisite breakfast. The coffee alone was of surpassing excellence. After breakfast, I waddled to the front desk and checked out, cringing only a touch at the bill. The hotel was pricey but the first act was priceless.

The Shenandoah Valley runs in a north-south direction between the Blue Ridge and Appalachian Mountains in western Virginia. These are the oldest mountains on the continent, born in a rift with the earth a billion years ago.

The two forks of the Shenandoah River conjoin above Massanutten Mountain, a rock formation three thousand feet tall and forty miles long set in the middle of the valley, like Devil's Tower on steroids. The unified river continues north to Harper's Ferry, where it joins the Potomac River, which joins the Chesapeake, which joins the ocean. Everything flows everywhere. And now I was flowing with it.

The origin of the name Shenandoah is hidden in mystery. Some suspect the name refers to a lost tribe, the Senedos, who disappeared from the valley long ago. The name is translated in several ways. The most popular interpretation is Daughter of the Stars. I prefer Silver Water.

I followed Highway 81 which followed the south fork of the Shenandoah River through the eastern part of the valley. North didn't seem backwards this time, maybe because we were both flowing home.

Suddenly I had a visitor. A hawk landed on the highway shoulder just in front of me. I had never heard of a raptor landing like that, flat on the ground on the side of a busy highway with no prey in sight. Yet there he was. Taller than the steel guardrail, he looked enormous, and very much like the hawk that led me out of Pipestone.

In a blip, I was past him. In a blur, he was gone. I looked for him in the rear view mirror. He had vanished.

Cruising up the valley, guided by Silver Water, Mozart quintets, and the handsome splendors of autumn, I was content. Years before I had visited the caverns of the Shenandoah—Luray and Endless—souvenirs of yet another ancient sea. I dismissed them now. Subterranean worlds no longer beckoned me.

Angling east across Virginia, I-66 carried me into home territory. I cut through Leesburg, then took White's Ferry across the Potomac River into Maryland, following familiar paths to familiar places, until finally I pulled up outside my home. Bernard and I waited in the car for a while.

Maryland is the Green state. But I had never noticed the colors of my home before: the key lime of the house itself, the dark Christmas of the evergreen trees flanking the door, the waxy green of the shrubs on either side, and the myriad emeralds of the grasses.

I looked at myself in the rearview mirror. Then I turned to Bernard and said:

"We're home. And everything looks different."

*
*
*

Circles begins this way:

> *"THE EYE is the first circle; the horizon which it forms is the second; and throughout nature this primary picture is repeated without end. It is the highest emblem in the cipher of the world. St. Augustine described the nature of God as a circle whose centre was everywhere and its circumference nowhere. We are all our lifetime reading the copious sense of this first of forms. One moral we have already deduced in considering the circular or compensatory character of every human action. Another analogy we shall now trace, that every action admits of being outdone. Our life is an apprenticeship to the truth that around every circle another can be drawn; that there is no end in nature, but every end is a beginning; that there is always another dawn risen on mid-noon, and under every deep a lower deep opens."*

STEPHEN EVANS

Afterword Part II

The cast iron gates, pearl-finished by flurries, were flung wide. Behind me on Lexington Road, tires grumbled white noise through the slush.

I took one step through the gates. The noise diminished. Even the sound of my breathing, labored in the cold, seemed swallowed by the frozen air. If this silence lasted an eternity, I thought, here was an audience that would appreciate.

The snow was wispy and dry. Barely half an inch powdered the road into the grounds of Sleepy Hollow Cemetery. Yet all colors had turned to white. The evergreen braches bowed under icy plumes. A slight breeze raised a miniature cyclone, lace-delicate fleeting spirit, that beckoned. I followed the white whorl.

No tracks disturbed the gleaming white path, which itself was barely distinguishable from the acres of alabaster waves. Regretting my footprints in the unstained road, I walked a few paces inward. The way wound left. I kept on straight. Authors Ridge was up. The high ground lay in the center. And somewhere in the deep heart of Concord, Ralph Waldo Emerson lay at rest.

I soon found and climbed slippery steps to the flat of a hill. The path, dusted white under swaying trees, was marked on either side by stones. A way down I knelt in the snow. The small headstone was worn almost smooth. Offering of flowers and notes, branches and stones, lay uncovered somehow in the snow. The marker had one word only: Henry.

Farther down, I passed Nathaniel Hawthorne on the left, and the Alcotts (Louisa May and Father Bronson) on the right, modest headstones, though larger than Thoreau's.

The path turned right. Here finally was the burial place of Ralph Waldo Emerson. A short white fence surrounded the plot, almost disappearing in the snow. A massive stone had been rolled into place, or had stood immovable even then. In the center of the stone, a plaque was embedded, partly obscured, the brass tarnished blue-green and unreadable.

I was reminded that in their lifetimes, Emerson was the world-famous sage. Thoreau was known to outsiders as that odd friend of Mr. Emerson. Now it was mostly the reverse. There were no offerings or remembrances here.

Standing by the grave, I had the curious urge to speak, a weird hope that I would be spoken to. But no words disturbed the preternatural tranquility.

After a few silent moments, I turned and left, tracing my footprints in reverse as I stepped down Authors Ridge. Some lines of verse came to mind, all at once and complete. I kept repeating them over and over so I wouldn't forget them.

In the car, a copy of Emerson's *Representative Men* lay on the seat, its shrink-wrap covering still intact over the black dust jacket. I had bought it an hour before at the gift shop at Walden, planning to read it that night. Pushing it aside, I pulled out my notebook and wrote the words I had been given:

I looked for footprints,
sure each step had shaped the earth,
and found the earth enfolding them instead.
As I left, I noticed my own footprints,
nearly covered by wind and snow,

but still enough to follow to the road.
This must be how they shaped the earth,
I thought, with footprints
just deep enough to point the way.

It was some weeks later when I finally opened *Representative Men* and read this:

Not a foot steps into the snow or along the ground, but prints, in characters more or less lasting, a map of its march.

Notes

I have read and benefited from many biographies of Emerson, but my favorites are *Ralph Waldo Emerson* by Oliver Wendell Holmes Sr. and *Emerson: The Mind on Fire* by Robert D. Richardson Jr. (who was also kind enough to buy this book).

Most of Emerson's works are in print and easily available. Many are available online.

STEPHEN EVANS

Acknowledgements

Many thanks to the generous and talented friends who have helped with this book, including Liv Blumer, Fred Ramey, Rosy Cole, Izzy Ballard, and Amanda Larson.

STEPHEN EVANS

About the Author

Stephen Evans is playwright and author. Find him online at:

https://www.istephenevans.com/

https://www.facebook.com/iStephenEvans

https://twitter.com/iStephenEvans

STEPHEN EVANS

Books by Stephen Evans

Fiction:

The Marriage of True Minds

Let Me Count the Ways

The Island of Always

Two Short Novels

Painting Sunsets

The Mind of a Writer and other Fables

Non-Fiction:

A Transcendental Journey

Funny Thing Is: A Guide to Understanding Comedy

The Laughing String: Thoughts on Writing

Layers of Life

Liebestraum

STEPHEN EVANS

Plays:

The Ghost Writer

Spooky Action at a Distance

Tourists

Generations (with Morey Norkin and Michael Gilles)

The Visitation Quartet

Verse:

Sonets from the Chesapeke

A Look from Winter

Limerosity

Limerositus

STEPHEN EVANS

STEPHEN EVANS

www.ingramcontent.com/pod-product-compliance
Lightning Source LLC
Chambersburg PA
CBHW021440070526
44577CB00002B/231